WOOTTON

ENDPAPER

High above Lebanon's Bekaa valley, Israeli and Syrian jets battle it out during the undeclared war of June 1982. In the foreground three American-built F-15 fighters of the Israeli Air Force fly high cover as a pair of Israeli Kfir fighter-bombers come in lower to attack surface-to-air missile sites, two of which have already been hit and are burning. In the distance three Syrian MiGs, struck by Israeli air-to-air missiles, plunge in flames to the valley floor. This oil painting is by famed British aviation artist Frank Wootton.

FIGHTING JETS

Other Publications:
THE CIVIL WAR
PLANET EARTH
COLLECTOR'S LIBRARY OF THE CIVIL WAR
LIBRARY OF HEALTH
CLASSICS OF THE OLD WEST
THE GOOD COOK
THE SEAFARERS
THE ENCYCLOPEDIA OF COLLECTIBLES
THE GREAT CITIES
WORLD WAR II
HOME REPAIR AND IMPROVEMENT
THE WORLD'S WILD PLACES
THE TIME-LIFE LIBRARY OF BOATING
HUMAN BEHAVIOR
THE ART OF SEWING
THE OLD WEST
THE EMERGENCE OF MAN
THE AMERICAN WILDERNESS
THE TIME-LIFE ENCYCLOPEDIA OF GARDENING
LIFE LIBRARY OF PHOTOGRAPHY
THIS FABULOUS CENTURY
FOODS OF THE WORLD
TIME-LIFE LIBRARY OF AMERICA
TIME-LIFE LIBRARY OF ART
GREAT AGES OF MAN
LIFE SCIENCE LIBRARY
THE LIFE HISTORY OF THE UNITED STATES
TIME READING PROGRAM
LIFE NATURE LIBRARY
LIFE WORLD LIBRARY

FAMILY LIBRARY:
HOW THINGS WORK IN YOUR HOME
THE TIME-LIFE BOOK OF THE FAMILY CAR
THE TIME-LIFE FAMILY LEGAL GUIDE
THE TIME-LIFE BOOK OF FAMILY FINANCE

*This volume is one of a series that traces the adventure and
science of aviation, from the earliest manned balloon ascension
through the era of jet flight.*

FIGHTING JETS

by Bryce Walker

AND THE EDITORS OF TIME-LIFE BOOKS

TIME-LIFE BOOKS, ALEXANDRIA, VIRGINIA

Time-Life Books Inc.
is a wholly owned subsidiary of

TIME INCORPORATED

FOUNDER: Henry R. Luce 1898-1967

Editor-in-Chief: Henry Anatole Grunwald
President: J. Richard Munro
Chairman of the Board: Ralph P. Davidson
Executive Vice President: Clifford J. Grum
Editorial Director: Ralph Graves
Group Vice President, Books: Joan D. Manley

TIME-LIFE BOOKS INC.

EDITOR: George Constable
Executive Editor: George Daniels
Director of Design: Louis Klein
Board of Editors: Dale M. Brown, Thomas A. Lewis,
Martin Mann, Robert G. Mason, Gerry Schremp,
Gerald Simons, Rosalind Stubenberg, Kit van Tulleken
Director of Administration: David L. Harrison
Director of Research: Carolyn L. Sackett
Director of Photography: John Conrad Weiser

PRESIDENT: Reginald K. Brack Jr.
Executive Vice President: John Steven Maxwell
Vice Presidents: George Artandi, Stephen L. Bair,
Peter G. Barnes, Nicholas Benton, John L. Canova,
Beatrice T. Dobie, Christopher T. Linen, James L. Mercer,
Paul R. Stewart

THE EPIC OF FLIGHT

EDITOR: Dale M. Brown
Designer: Van W. Carney
Chief Researcher: W. Mark Hamilton

Editorial Staff for *Fighting Jets*

Associate Editors: Lee Hassig, Ellen Phillips (text);
Robin Richman (pictures)
Staff Writers: Kevin D. Armstrong, Deborah Berger-Turnbull,
Rachel Cox, Glenn Martin McNatt, Robert Menaker
Researchers: LaVerle Berry, Roxie France, Anne Munoz-
Furlong, B. Jean Strong
Assistant Designer: Anne K. DuVivier
Copy Coordinators: Stephen G. Hyslop, Anthony K. Pordes
Picture Coordinator: Renée DeSandies
Editorial Assistant: Constance B. Strawbridge

Editorial Operations
Design: Arnold C. Holeywell (assistant director);
Anne B. Landry (art coordinator);
James J. Cox (quality control)
Research: Jane Edwin (assistant director), Louise D. Forstall
Copy Room: Susan Galloway Goldberg (director),
Celia Beattie
Production: Feliciano Madrid (director), Gordon E. Buck,
Peter Inchauteguiz

Correspondents: Elisabeth Kraemer (Bonn); Margot
Hapgood, Dorothy Bacon (London); Miriam Hsia, Lucy T.
Voulgaris (New York); Maria Vincenza Aloisi, Josephine du
Brusle (Paris); Ann Natanson (Rome). Valuable assistance
was also provided by: Robert Wurmstedt (Cairo); Martin
Levin (Jerusalem); Felix Rosenthal (Moscow); Christina
Lieberman, Cornelis Verwaal (New York).

THE AUTHOR

Bryce Walker, a former Time-Life Books editor, worked closely with U.S. Air Force historians, technical experts and combat pilots in producing the manuscript for *Fighting Jets.* He was a writer on military affairs for *Stars and Stripes* while serving in Korea in 1960 and was a reporter at the Panmunjom talks. He has written three other volumes for Time-Life Books—*The Great Divide, The Armada* and *Earthquake.*

THE CONSULTANTS

Walter J. Boyne is the Director of the National Air and Space Museum, Washington, D.C. He enlisted in the U.S. Air Force in 1951 and retired as a colonel in 1974, with more than 5,000 flying hours in a score of aircraft, including the B-50, B-47 and B-52. Among his recent published works is *Boeing B-52: A Documentary History.*

Donald S. Lopez is Chairman of the Aeronautics Department of the National Air and Space Museum. He holds a master's degree in aeronautics from the California Institute of Technology. After serving with the Air Force until 1964, he spent eight years as a systems engineer on the Apollo-Saturn launch vehicle and the Skylab orbital workshop before joining the Smithsonian Institution in 1972.

For information about any Time-Life book, please write:
Reader Information
Time-Life Books
541 North Fairbanks Court
Chicago, Illinois 60611

First printing.
Printed in U.S.A.
Published simultaneously in Canada.
School and library distribution by Silver Burdett
Company, Morristown, New Jersey.

TIME-LIFE is a trademark of Time Incorporated U.S.A.

Library of Congress Cataloguing in Publication Data
Walker, Bryce
    Fighting jets.
    (The Epic of flight)
    Bibliography: p.
    Includes index.
    1. Jet planes, Military—History. 2. Air warfare—
History.   I. Time-Life Books.   II. Title.   III. Series.
UG1240.W34   1983   358.4'183'09   83-532
ISBN 0-8094-3362-1
ISBN 0-8094-3363-X (lib. bdg.)

CONTENTS

A new era of combat

On August 27, 1939, just four days before the outbreak of World War II, a slender, unconventional research airplane designated the Heinkel 178 took off from Marienhe Airfield in Germany to make the first successful flight of a turbojet aircraft. The event, although hardly noticed at the time, marked the dawn of a new age in aerial warfare.

It was a revolution created basically by two men— Frank Whittle of Great Britain and Hans von Ohain of Germany. Their radical theories regarding aircraft propulsion stirred little interest at first, but war inevitably prompted a reassessment. By 1944, Germany, desperate for a means of halting the Allied bombing offensive, had a dazzling operational jet in the Messerschmitt 262 *(right)*. And Great Britain, the United States and Japan each developed and flew jet fighters before the War ended.

Although the first fighting jets had little effect on the outcome of that conflict, their appearance set the stage for future generations of jet warplanes—aircraft that would play a vital role in determining the fate of contending nations. The dramatic views on these and the following pages, painted by some of the world's leading aviation artists, depict highlights in the 40-year evolution of this awesome weapon.

The hunter becomes the hunted in this vivid portrayal of Luftwaffe General Adolf Galland's last combat, painted by British aviation artist Frank Wootton. Attacking a formation of Allied bombers over Germany in April 1945, Galland was jumped by American P-47 fighters, which riddled his Me 262 jet with bullets and seriously wounded the German ace.

Trailing smoke, a North Korean Yak-15 fighter goes down in flames before the guns of a U.S. Marine Corps F3D all-weather interceptor piloted by Major William Stratton on the night of November 3, 1952. Painted by American artist R. G. Smith, the scene commemorates the first downing of an enemy jet aircraft by a radar-equipped American jet.

U.S. Navy A-4s fly over the carrier U.S.S. Enterprise, stationed off the coast of North Vietnam, in R. G. Smith's rendition of a combat mission. The carrier belonged to Task Force 77, which was part of the U.S. Seventh Fleet in the Pacific.

A swirling high-speed dogfight between a North Vietnamese MiG-17 and a U.S. Navy F-4 Phantom piloted by Commander Denny Wisely ends badly for the Communist jet. The action, which occurred on April 24, 1967, was meticulously re-created from the pilot's own account by R. G. Smith.

Russian tanks advance under a screen of wheeling MiG-27 tactical fighters during a joint training exercise in the Soviet Union. American artist William Phillips depicted the MiGs armed for close air support: a 23-mm. Gatling-type gun, heat-seeking Atoll air-to-air missiles and a 550-pound cluster bomb beneath each wing.

A British Aerospace Harrier, the world's first operational jet fighter with vectored thrust for vertical takeoffs and landings, lifts off in a combat mode from a concealed location. Frank Wootton painted the scene to illustrate the Harrier's ability to operate from remote areas and in almost any kind of terrain.

A U.S. Air Force KC-10 jet tanker refuels an F-15 Eagle fighter at 30,000 feet in this view, painted from the perspective of the wingman's cockpit by R. G. Smith. Air-to-air refueling enables American fighting jets to fly nonstop to trouble spots anywhere in the world within hours.

1
The Nazi wonderbird

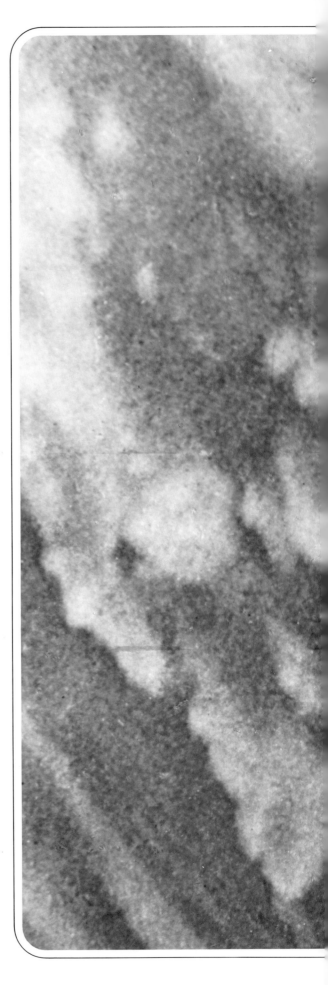

The weather was perfect for high-altitude photoreconnaissance. Flight Lieutenant A. E. Wall of the Royal Air Force guided his twin-engined de Havilland Mosquito along an arrow-straight course 30,000 feet above the neatly plotted landscape of southern Germany. His cameras, clicking automatically, would record the smallest details for later analysis in England. To the south, high above the Bavarian Alps, great stacks of cumulus had begun to build. No matter, Wall thought, they might prove useful as cover in the event of interception by German fighters.

There seemed little chance of that, however. Wall had flown 600 miles from England and had seen no sign of the once-mighty Luftwaffe. It was July 25, 1944, one year before the end of the War, and everywhere the forces of Hitler's Reich were in retreat. A massive invasion force commanded by General Dwight D. Eisenhower was pushing through France in the West, and in the East the Red Army was grinding steadily forward. A perpetual stream of Allied bombers—American Liberators and Flying Fortresses by day, British Lancasters and Halifaxes by night—was systematically pulverizing Germany's cities and factories. Allied fighters had all but swept the Luftwaffe from the sky.

Suddenly, as Wall approached Munich, his navigator barked out a warning: enemy aircraft 400 yards astern. The navigator could not identify the plane, but it seemed to have come from nowhere, moving in fast on the Mosquito's tail. Instantly, Wall nosed down, sending the Mosquito into a shallow power dive, and shoved his throttles forward.

The reconnaissance version of the Mosquito fighter-bomber, stripped of weapons to save weight, was one of the Allies' fastest aircraft. In a dive at full throttle, the plane had reached 412 miles per hour and was still accelerating. Wall should have been able to pull away from almost any German fighter. But not this one. It streaked in like avenging lightning, faster than any airborne object he had ever encountered. It passed overhead, banked sharply and seconds later appeared again on his tail.

Wall heaved the nimble Mosquito into a steep left bank, then straightened out. The evasive maneuver failed. From behind came the thudding cadence of cannon fire. No hits. Again Wall broke desperately

A Messerschmitt 262, its twin jet engines outlined against the sky, pursues an American P-51 Mustang in this gun-camera photograph taken from a second P-51, which shot down the German fighter.

away, edging his stick back to regain altitude—and suddenly was free. The German, going too fast to follow the turn, sped off into the blue.

The RAF plane headed south, searching for cloud cover, but the enemy fighter was too swift. It swung back in a wide arc and closed again on the Mosquito's tail, cannon blazing from 800 yards. The range was too great, however, and the shots missed their mark. Wall swerved to shake off his assailant. Four more times the German drove in at a velocity that seemed incomprehensible, and the Englishman evaded with abrupt turns that the other plane was unable to follow. Once, with both aircraft locked in a tight descending spiral, Wall was able to swing behind the German, and might have scored a hit himself had he carried the guns to do so.

After nearly 15 minutes of deadly ballet, Wall reached the cloud banks over the Alps. Weaving and dodging with the German still on his tail, he dived into the protective cumulus. Three or four minutes later, when he emerged from the clouds, his pursuer was nowhere to be seen.

Wall had very nearly fallen victim to the fastest warplane yet to fly— the Messerschmitt 262. This single-seat fighter had a sleek, flat-bellied fuselage that resembled nothing so much as the body of a giant shark. Allied bombers were the Me 262's intended prey, and it had four 30-millimeter cannon, the largest caliber guns carried by any German fighter, with which to shoot them down. In fighting trim, it could travel at 540 miles per hour in level flight—a full 70 miles per hour faster than the speediest Allied fighter at the time, the latest model of America's P-47 Thunderbolt. Slung under the Me 262's sweptback wings was the secret of its power—two lozenge-shaped Junkers Jumo 004 turbojets, with a combined thrust of nearly 4,000 pounds.

The Jumo 004 was the first mass-produced jet engine. The piston engine had all but reached its limits; only by increasing its weight and complexity could more power be achieved. Such a course would be self-defeating—not just because the added weight would demand still more power to lift the engine skyward, but also because of a built-in limitation of the plane's propeller. For an aircraft to fly faster, its propeller must, of course, spin more rapidly; but the faster it spins, the closer the blade tips approach the speed of sound. The result is a maelstrom of turbulence that limits the propeller's ability to pull the plane forward.

The Jumo 004 had neither of these disadvantages. Compared with a piston engine, a turbojet is simplicity itself. It generates vast amounts of power for its size and weight. And although the turbines spin at thousands of revolutions per minute, they are smaller in diameter than propellers; with less distance to cover, the tips never come near to reaching the speed of sound. The one drawback of the Jumo 004—as in the other early jets—was its thirst for fuel: At low altitude, it could consume fuel at two or three times the rate of a piston engine.

Propelled by its pair of mighty turbojets, the Me 262 swept in a new era of flight. Though the plane arrived in the skies too late to change the course of the War for Germany, it showed an amazed world what a jet fighter could do. Following the collapse of Germany and Japan, nations rushed to arm themselves with their own versions of this new weapon. A race to develop and fly faster and yet faster jets began. And the wars that flared in subsequent years—Korea, Vietnam, the Arab-Israeli conflicts—became the proving grounds of ever swifter, ever more lethal aircraft. By 1953, jets had exceeded the speed of sound in level flight. Gradually, payloads increased. By the time of the 1950s' Cold War, the United States had harnessed eight jet engines to a giant bomber, the Boeing B-52, that not only outsped and outdistanced its World War II predecessors, but dwarfed them in the tons of bombs it could carry in its belly. Even more remarkable bombers would follow the B-52—both in the United States and in the Soviet Union.

As the years flashed by, jet technology steadily advanced. Fighter pilots would fly craft that boasted uncanny capabilities. Planes would dodge mountains automatically; they would acquire reserves of power so great that they could accelerate supersonically straight up, like a rocket; and they would unleash—or be the target of—weapons so deadly that a jet could be knocked from the sky before the man at the controls realized he was in danger.

The first rumblings of the jet revolution had begun a decade before the first Me 262 lifted off its runway in southern Germany. Back in the early 1930s a few farsighted engineers had been toying with the thought that a stream of hot exhaust from a gas turbine might be used to drive an aircraft. The advantages were obvious, but so were the problems. Such a device would weigh far too much to be carried in a plane, skeptics said. It would burn too much fuel to be efficient. Furthermore, the technology was still not safe. In the internal heat of jet fires, it was thought, the

During a test flight, a Heinkel 280 prototype, the world's first experimental jet fighter, climbs toward its estimated 37,000-foot ceiling. Heinkel built nine versions of the He 280, one of which reached 577 mph, before the Luftwaffe halted development in favor of the more heavily armed Me 262.

turbine blades would become brittle and break. But not everyone was so sure, and in a few small workshops in Germany, Italy and England, young scientists began to assemble experimental jet engines.

One of the first to do so was a young Royal Air Force officer, Frank Whittle, who had graduated with top honors in engineering from Cambridge University. With just £2,000 ($10,000) borrowed from friends, and a grudging go-ahead from his superiors in the RAF, he started piecing together a demonstration jet. The work went slowly; all the experts' predictions seemed to come true. Whittle's first test model ran so erratically that it almost blew up in the machine shop. Three and a half years went by before he succeeded in producing a workable engine, and even that did not develop enough power to propel a plane.

In Germany, another bright young engineer, Hans von Ohain, was having better luck. Ohain, urged on by his old engineering professor, had approached one of Germany's most innovative aircraft manufacturers, Ernst Heinkel, with plans for an experimental jet engine. Heinkel listened intently as the young man spoke and then called in his top engineers for a technical opinion. By April 1936 Ohain was working away in a secluded shop at Heinkel's plant in Warnemünde, north of Berlin. Within a year he had a viable engine.

Officials in Germany's Air Ministry, subordinate to the Luftwaffe since 1935, were aware of Ohain's work, and convinced of its importance, they took a fateful step. In 1938, they asked several of Germany's foremost engine manufacturers—among them Junkers and Bavarian Motor Works (BMW)—to develop turbojets of their own. And for the fighter planes these new engines were to power, the Air Ministry turned to two of Germany's leading aircraft designers. One was Heinkel, who they knew was building a single-purpose airplane for testing Ohain's engine. The other was Heinkel's archrival, Willy Messerschmitt, the brilliant designer of the Me 109. For the next several years these two men would be locked in a struggle, compounded by severe technical problems and alternating degrees of official interference and neglect, to produce the first operational fighting jet.

By the summer of 1939, Ohain had refined his engine to the point where it was ready to power an airplane. Heinkel, meanwhile, had completed the test-bed: He labeled it the He 178. On August 27, 1939, with Ohain's engine pushing it along, the He 178 rolled down a test runway and lifted into the air. It made a single circuit of the airfield and returned to earth. Jet propulsion had become a fact.

Astonishingly, few people seemed to take much notice. Exactly five days after the He 178's maiden flight, Hitler's Wehrmacht stormed across the border into Poland, thereby launching the bloodiest war in history. In the fires of the Blitzkrieg, Heinkel's pioneering feat was all but forgotten. Furthermore, covering the ground troops and spearheading the assault were nearly 1,600 prop-driven Luftwaffe fighters and light bombers, power enough to seize quick and total control of Polish airspace. Victory was inevitable; Poland collapsed within the month. With

Reich Marshal Hermann Göring (center) confers with aircraft designer Willy Messerschmitt in February 1941, during the planning phase of the Me 262. At Göring's right is General Ernst Udet, the Luftwaffe's procurement chief and a powerful promoter of earlier Messerschmitt planes.

such aerial might already in its arsenal, what need had Germany for some propellerless plane whose usefulness was still unproved? Two months later the Luftwaffe's chief of procurement, General Ernst Udet, was persuaded to watch a demonstration flight of Heinkel's new jet. As the plane went through its paces, Udet could barely stifle a yawn.

Contributing to the Luftwaffe's lack of interest was an obvious limitation in the He 178's performance. In its best flight, the Heinkel jet had reached a top speed of 435 miles per hour, but Ohain's engine was proving to be a prodigious fuel guzzler. The He 178 could stay in the air for only 10 minutes at a time. Eventually, the jet's performance could be improved; Udet, however, was interested in the here and now.

Nonetheless, work proceeded on the two jet-fighter prototypes commissioned by the Air Ministry. Heinkel was the first into the air, with the innovative He 280. Among its notable features was a tricycle landing gear, in which the third wheel supported the nose instead of the tail. This arrangement lowered the nose, allowing the pilot to see ahead while taxiing, and made the aircraft easier to land in a crosswind. The He 280 also introduced the world's first ejection seat, designed to blast the pilot clear of the cockpit with a charge of compressed air. On April 2, 1941, near Rostock on the Baltic Sea, the jet made its maiden flight, a successful though unremarkable low-altitude circuit of the field.

The main reason Heinkel beat Messerschmitt into the air was that neither Junkers nor BMW was able to deliver its engines on schedule. Heinkel solved this problem by installing his own engine—an advance on Ohain's demonstration model. Messerschmitt had no such option.

The Messerschmitt fighter was being developed specifically to accommodate the new engine from BMW. But BMW's engineers kept running into problems. The thrust was inadequate, they said, and they had to enlarge the turbines. So Messerschmitt revised his plans to allow for the extra size and weight. By early 1941 he was ready with the new design, but BMW, blaming further technical difficulties, had not yet produced the engine. Messerschmitt waited until April and then started testing his airframe with a conventional piston engine installed in the nose.

Still the months went by, and it was November before the BMW turbines arrived. The designer fitted them under the wings, as planned, painstakingly ground-tested them, and by March 1942 felt confident that they could carry his airplane into the sky. Nevertheless, some cautionary inner voice told him that, for this first jet flight, he had better keep the piston engine too, just in case. It was lucky he did. The Me 262 went hurtling down the runway, its two jets howling and its propeller spinning furiously. No sooner had the plane left the ground than first the port and

Exhaust fumes pour from the engines of the Me 262V3 moments before its first successful test flight, on July 18, 1942, at Leipheim, Germany. After a 12-minute flight in which he reached 448 mph, pilot Fritz Wendel reported that the plane's Jumo 004 turbojets "ran like clockwork."

then the starboard jet flamed out. With only a single prop for power, Fritz Wendel, Messerschmitt's chief test pilot, was barely able to coax the lumbering, overloaded aircraft back to a safe landing.

Unwilling to wait for BMW to revise the design of its engine, Messerschmitt turned to a more promising turbine, the Jumo 004, being perfected by Junkers. The Jumo jets were even bigger and heavier than the BMWs, and this called for still further adjustments in design. One change was to angle back the wings, thus balancing the added weight. This gave the jet a serendipitous bonanza in performance. At high velocities, the sweptback wings countered the speed-robbing effects of compressibility, a phenomenon that greatly increases air resistance near the sound barrier, and so boosted the new jet's speed. At last, more than a year after the He 280 took to the air, the Me 262 was ready for flight.

On July 18, 1942, Wendel started down the runway at Leipheim, near Messerschmitt's Augsburg plant, and throttled up to 112 miles per hour, the anticipated speed for lift-off. The airstrip was only 3,600 feet long, but Wendel believed it was long enough. He eased the stick forward to raise the tail and . . . nothing! The Me 262 clung stubbornly to earth, careering along like a runaway truck. What was wrong?

Unlike the He 280, the Me 262 employed a landing gear with a tail wheel that tilted the nose skyward and directed the exhaust from the engines downward. As Wendel accelerated, the exhaust bounced off the runway toward the tail, and the turbulence it created disrupted the smooth flow of air past the tail and canceled the effect of the elevators— the control surfaces that raise or lower the tail. The same thing had no doubt happened when Wendel had tested the BMW-powered version. But the airstream from the prop had counteracted the effects of the jet exhaust on the tail, allowing the aircraft to take off.

Wendel pulled back the throttles and braked to a halt mere yards from the runway's end. He climbed from the cockpit and huddled briefly with Messerschmitt engineers, who gave him an idea. Wendel climbed back into the cockpit and headed down the runway a second time. At 112 miles per hour he touched the brakes in a single, sudden jab. The airplane bucked, and the force of this movement kicked the tail smartly upward. Seconds later the Me 262 was circling the airfield in swift, swooping arcs. Wendel stayed aloft for 12 minutes and returned to land. He was scarcely able to control his excitement. This new machine, he reported, "was a sheer pleasure to fly." Yet Wendel could easily have killed himself: Had he misjudged the application of the brakes, the jet could have tipped onto its nose. Emboldened, Wendel took the plane up six more times. Messerschmitt felt that the time was now ripe to have the Luftwaffe try the jet for itself.

On August 17, 1942, Heinrich Beauvais, a civilian engineer and test pilot for the Luftwaffe, arrived at the Messerschmitt plant to fly the new plane. Wendel explained to Beauvais how to ease the throttles forward to keep the engines from erupting in flames because of a sudden excess of fuel. He also described the unorthodox procedure for getting the jet

Before making his first flight in the Me 262 on May 22, 1943, Luftwaffe fighter chief Major General Adolf Galland (right) confers with test pilot Fritz Wendel. After the flight, Galland urged his superiors to halt production of the propeller-driven Me 109 fighter in favor of the 262.

off the ground. As Beauvais taxied the Me 262 to takeoff position, Wendel stationed himself next to the runway, about 325 yards from the end, at the point where Beauvais would have to jab the brakes. Advancing the throttles, Beauvais began his takeoff roll. When he passed Wendel, however, it was clear that the Me 262 was traveling too slowly. Instead of stopping the plane, Beauvais tried to raise the tail. It lifted momentarily, then settled back onto the runway. Beauvais stopped the jet, taxied back to the end of the runway and tried a second time, with the same results. On the third try, as he hurtled along the airstrip, the jet became ever so slightly airborne. But Beauvais was not climbing fast enough. Seconds later, the wheels cut a swath through a field; then the right wing tip clipped a manure pile, spinning the plane around as it pancaked to the ground. Beauvais emerged from the cockpit shaken. The jet, though badly damaged, was eventually rebuilt to fly again.

Despite Beauvais's experience, the Luftwaffe remained interested in the Me 262. Other test pilots, having mastered the takeoff in later prototypes, began to probe the plane's capabilities. Soon they were pushing it to 530 miles per hour. At this unheard-of speed, they found it amazingly maneuverable. In October Field Marshal Erhard Milch, who had succeeded Udet as the Luftwaffe's head of procurement, authorized Messerschmitt to build 17 Me 262s for operational evaluation.

Heinkel, meanwhile, was running into difficulties with the He 280. Though a dream to fly, it was—at 491 miles per hour—slower than the Me 262. Heinkel was certain that with more powerful engines, the He 280 could catch up with the rival plane. But bigger engines would only exacerbate a more serious shortcoming. The He 280 was severely limited in its fuel capacity. Consequently, its range was two thirds that of the earliest Me 262s, and more powerful engines would only consume fuel faster and shorten range even more. To add larger fuel tanks would mean redesigning the jet virtually from scratch.

In the rival camp, trials of the Me 262 continued through the autumn and winter of 1942. By early 1943, the jet was reaching the astonishing speed of 590 miles per hour in a shallow dive. That seemed to represent the upper limit of velocity. Pilots dared not go beyond it, for at that speed, as the plane approached the sound barrier, it began to pitch and shudder in a manner that made it virtually uncontrollable.

By now, the War was going badly for the Germans. They were fighting on two fronts—against the Russians in the East, and the British and the Americans in North Africa. The Allies were dropping thousands of tons of bombs on the factories, dams and bridges of Germany's industrial Ruhr Valley, and on the ancient Rhineland cities. As the tides of battle shifted, the German High Command began to vacillate. No one seemed able to make a firm decision. Priorities were set, and orders were issued, and then a few weeks or months later everything would be canceled or reversed. In this uncertain climate, the prospect that Messerschmitt's new jet fighter would ever be put into production seemed bleak.

About the only constant in this period was Hitler's newfound antipathy toward fighter planes of any sort. Early in the War, they had been the cutting edge for his victories; now that the Allies were winning, he saw fighters as essentially defensive weapons, to be used for clearing enemy intruders from the skies. And to Hitler, defense sounded too much like defeat. What the Führer wanted was new and better bombers. With bombers he could go on the offensive—hit enemy fortifications, resume his air attacks on London and avenge the insult of the bombing raids on the Ruhr and Rhineland.

The upper echelons of the Luftwaffe held an opposing view—at least among themselves. Without a strong fighter defense to relieve the pressure of Allied bombing on Germany's aircraft industry, they believed, the idea of a bomber offensive was absurd. Yet Hitler's underlings hesitated to debate him on this or any other issue. Shortly after the bomber raids started, he had gone into a screaming tantrum in which he accused the Luftwaffe of letting him down—a charge that carried with it the threat of dismissal, or worse, for the Luftwaffe leadership.

Luftwaffe chief Hermann Göring remained silent on the question of fighters versus bombers. The Air Ministry was equally cowed, and Field Marshal Milch was ready to see to it that the German aircraft industry produced whatever Hitler wanted.

Among the strongest proponents of the Me 262 was one of the Luftwaffe's boldest and most charismatic aces, Major General Adolf Galland. Dashing, brusque, unflappable, his peaked cap tilted rakishly across his brow and a black cigar perpetually clenched in his teeth, he radiated assurance and vitality. His progress through the ranks had been nothing short of meteoric. At the age of 30, with more than 90 air victories to his credit, he had become Germany's youngest general and was put in charge of the Luftwaffe's fighters.

In his years of combat in Europe, Galland had seen firsthand a steady rise in the skill and numbers of his British and American opponents. Now he began receiving intelligence reports of an enormous build-up of American bombers and fighter escorts at air bases in England. He watched in alarm as the Luftwaffe forces were stretched thin across multiplying battlefronts. Unless Germany's scanty air defenses were strengthened, and quickly, they would soon be overwhelmed. A new kind of aircraft was needed, said Galland, "with better performance to be superior to the enemy's." He had in mind the Me 262; soon he would get a chance to try it out for himself.

On May 22, 1943, he paid a visit to the Messerschmitt flight-test center at Lechfeld, near the main Messerschmitt plant at Augsburg. Parked at the end of the runway were two Me 262s, looking, he thought, "like silver streaks on the horizon." Galland watched a demonstration flight and was given a quick briefing on the plane's handling characteristics; then he climbed into the cockpit of the second jet. He ran up the engines and started down the runway. With a deft tap of the brakes he kicked the tail off the ground, and in seconds the Me 262 rose into the sky, carrying its pilot into a new dimension: "For the first time," Galland recalled after the War, "I was flying by jet propulsion! No engine vibrations. No torque and no lashing sound of the propeller. Accompanied by a whistling sound, my jet shot through the air."

A prop-driven supply plane happened to be flying over the field, and in the exuberance of the moment Galland banked toward it in mock attack. As he swooped and turned, he marveled at how fast and responsive the jet was. With such an airplane, his fighter pilots would have a commanding advantage over any opponent. On landing, Galland thought to himself: "This is not a step forward; this is a leap!"

Galland fired off a telegram to Milch. "The Me 262 is a tremendous stroke of fortune for us," he wrote. "It will guarantee us an unbelievable advantage in operations, so long as the enemy sticks to piston propulsion. It opens up entirely new possibilities in tactics."

Galland's enthusiastic endorsement of the Me 262 betrayed an underlying sense of urgency. If the enemy beat Germany into service with its own jet fighter, the advantages of the Me 262 might well be neutralized. The Germans knew of Frank Whittle's prewar experiments with a jet engine, but they did not know whether the British had produced an airworthy craft. Actually, the Germans had little to fear.

Whittle's work had begun to attract government attention after 1937, but development of the turbojet had been handed over to Britain's premier engine manufacturer, Rolls-Royce. Not until May 1941 did a small experimental plane, built by the Gloster Aircraft Company and designated the E 28/39, take to the air. The test so impressed Air Ministry officials that they ordered up a full-scale prototype jet fighter. Called the Gloster Meteor, it was a twin-engined, single-seat interceptor superficially similar to the Me 262. But because of greater drag and less powerful engines, it was 100 miles per hour slower; it was also less

The Luftwaffe's deadly "powered egg"

Allied bomber crews flying over Germany in the summer of 1944 encountered a new enemy fighter that was even faster than the jet-propelled Messerschmitt 262. The diminutive interceptor, the Messerschmitt 163 Komet, had short, sweptback wings of wood; a stubby, egg-shaped metal fuselage; and a revolutionary 3,750-pound-thrust rocket motor that blasted it through the sky at nearly 600 mph.

The Komet, like the Me 262, was one of Germany's so-called wonder weapons unveiled during the final year of the War. But any resemblance between the two ended there. Dubbed the "powered egg" by Luftwaffe test pilots, the Komet exhausted its 437-gallon fuel supply within four to seven minutes after takeoff, which limited its radius of action to 25 miles. Climbing straight up at 11,810 feet a minute, it would rise above Allied bomber formations, nose over and dive to the attack, raking the intruders with its twin 30-mm. cannon. As soon as the rocket motor quit, the pilot broke off and glided back to base.

The plane had a serious flaw, however. Its fuel, a mixture of methyl alcohol and concentrated hydrogen peroxide, was so volatile that it was liable to explode on the slightest provocation. A number of Komets simply blew up on the runway. Others suffered engine failures that filled the cockpit with acrid fumes, blinding the pilot; one unfortunate flier, doused with the highly corrosive chemicals from ruptured fuel lines, literally dissolved in his seat.

Of the 279 Komets manufactured during the War, only a handful saw combat, claiming nine victories over Allied bombers. "It was ten years ahead of its time, but the stress of war accelerated its development," recalled Luftwaffe test pilot Mano Ziegler, "and because of that, it was probably also the most dangerous aircraft ever built."

Workers at Peenemünde on Germany's Baltic coast tow an Me 163B Komet off the runway after lifting it onto a dolly fitted with air cushions.

Trailing a plume of white vapor, an Me 163A prototype flashes over Peenemünde during a low-altitude speed run in 1941.

heavily armed, carrying only 20-millimeter cannon compared with the 30-millimeter weapons on the German plane. The Meteor flew for the first time on March 5, 1943, from an airfield at Boscombe Down.

A couple of months after the Meteor's debut, British intelligence began uncovering ominous signs that Germany was indeed far ahead in developing an operational jet fighter. Air-reconnaissance photographs of an airfield at Peenemünde near the Baltic revealed strange sets of parallel scorch marks, similar to those made by the hot exhaust of the Gloster Meteor on takeoff. They were made by the Me 262. As photo interpreters sifted through their files, they found photographs taken months earlier that showed the German jet's unmistakable spoor—at Peenemünde, and at Leipheim and Lechfeld near the Messerschmitt factories as well. Here was cause for real concern. With that much lead in testing, the German jet might become operational any day.

In Germany, Galland was as excited as the British were uneasy. His enthusiasm for the Me 262 infected Göring and Milch. With their endorsement, the Air Ministry decided in early June to rush the jet into production. The following month, Göring paid a visit to Lechfeld to watch the Me 262 in flight. By now, a tricycle undercarriage had been fitted to the craft, solving the takeoff problem by directing the exhaust away from the ground. Göring was thoroughly taken with the jet, and he sent a glowing report to Hitler.

Hitler was not impressed. The Führer had totally lost confidence in the Luftwaffe. He blamed Göring for failing to slow the Allied bombing raids, and for fumbling an airlift of supplies to the German Sixth Army at Stalingrad, thus contributing to its defeat. A new heavy bomber, the He 177, had been promised for 1941; the deadline had passed more than 18 months earlier, but the plane was nowhere near completion. Enough was enough. Hitler declared that nothing would be done with the new fighter until he had weighed its merits. Testing could continue with only a few prototypes.

To help him decide about the plane, Hitler sent Göring to Messerschmitt with a question. Could the fighter be made into a bomber? There was no reason, of course, why turbojets could not be used to power bombers. Indeed, on June 15, 1943, Germany had flown the first prototype of a twin-engined jet bomber and reconnaissance aircraft called the Arado 234 *(page 32)*. This plane, however, was far behind the Me 262 in its development; Hitler could have his jet bomber sooner by converting the Messerschmitt. But here was a plane designed as a fast interceptor, a pure fighter that could cut through the rolling waves of Allied bomber groups and their fighter escorts. To encumber it with bombs and the apparatus needed for aiming and dropping them would drastically limit its performance. Hoping to put the matter to rest so that the aircraft could go into production as soon as possible, Messerschmitt said, "Provision has been made from the very first for installing two bomb racks." In fact, the designer had never contemplated putting bombs on the jet, though he knew it was possible.

Throughout its development, engineers used the Me 262 as a flying laboratory to test new weapons for the revolutionary jet. Among the more successful were 550-pound bombs installed on wing racks (top) and a row of 12 R4M rockets fitted on each wing (above). The rockets fired in rapid succession and were designed to saturate a target the size of a B-17.

In their rush to increase the 262's deadliness, German scientists produced some wildly impractical armament, including a nose cannon (top) and a towable 2,200-pound bomb (above). The 50-mm. cannon was unsuitable because it produced a blinding flash when fired. The bomb made the 262 unstable in flight and was scrapped after a few test runs.

And how long would it take to get them ready, asked Göring, "if we now have to proceed at a breakneck pace?"

"That can be done relatively quickly," Messerschmitt blandly answered, estimating two weeks. "It is merely a question of the fairing for the bomb racks." Göring seemed satisfied and departed in high spirits. Messerschmitt hoped to let the matter die, but it would not.

Soon afterward, the designer was ordered to prepare a demonstration of the jet for the Führer himself. On the appointed day Hitler stood beside the runway with Göring, Galland and other high officials and watched the Me 262 perform. He seemed favorably impressed. Turning to the Luftwaffe chief, he asked, "Can this aircraft carry bombs?"

"Yes, my Führer," Göring answered, then proceeded to expand upon what Messerschmitt had told him. "There is enough power to spare to carry 1,000 pounds, perhaps even 2,000 pounds."

That was all Hitler needed. Less than two weeks later he telegraphed Göring, stressing the "tremendous importance of the production of jet-propelled aircraft for employment as fighter-bombers." Hitler hoped the plane would be ready in time to repel the invasion he expected in the spring. "The decisive thing is to drop bombs on their heads the moment they land," he explained at a staff conference in Berlin. "That will force them to take cover, which will waste hours and hours."

Hitler's generals, convinced that their leader was making a terrible mistake, simply chose not to listen. Lacking a direct order to do otherwise, they would ignore the Führer's wishes and let the wheels grind on. Messerschmitt would gear up for production of the Me 262 with an immediate order for 60 fighters. To cover himself, he would assign a small group to come up with a way of arming the jet with bombs.

By the end of April 1944, enough fighters had been built to equip a small Luftwaffe training squadron at Lechfeld. Here Messerschmitt test pilots gave a cram course to experienced combat airmen on how to handle the new jets. Then the airmen were on their own. One of the squadron's tasks was to explore tactics that would exploit the jet's high speed and superior climbing performance. Another was to experiment with various weapon combinations and different attack formations. It was hoped that in the process any bugs in the fighter would be uncovered so they could be eliminated on the assembly line.

Hitler knew little of these developments. In the last week of May, he summoned Milch, Göring, Galland and others of the Luftwaffe's top echelon to the Eagle's Nest, his mountaintop retreat at Obersalzberg in Bavaria. The purpose of the meeting was an emergency review of Germany's air defense. For months now, swarms of British Lancaster and American B-17 and B-24 heavy bombers had been rumbling virtually unchallenged through Germany's airspace; even Berlin had been hit. Long-range P-47 Thunderbolt and P-51 Mustang fighters escorting the raiders outnumbered the defending Luftwaffe by an estimated 7 to 1. The losses had been devastating—1,000 aircraft in four months—and Galland had written his superiors "that the danger

The world's first jet bomber

Months before the revolutionary Me 262 made its maiden flight in July 1942, German engineers were already planning a bigger, more sophisticated jet—the Arado 234 high-level bomber. By 1941, work had started on the first of nearly three dozen prototypes.

The Arado's engineers incorporated a host of new features in the craft. To reduce drag and weight, they supplied several early models with a trolley that was jettisoned after takeoff *(right);* skids allowed the planes to land on grass. Other prototypes used rocket boosters for takeoffs from short runways. Some models contained such advanced features as a pressurized cabin and one of the first ejection seats. Others had four engines *(top right).*

In the summer of 1944, the twin-engined Arado 234 B—the Blitz—went into production. With a top speed of 461 mph and a ceiling of 33,000 feet, the Blitz *(below)* was years ahead of any Allied bomber. But it came too late to revive the fortunes of the moribund Reich.

Workers pull a four-engined Ar 234 C onto the runway prior to a test flight.

A twin-engined Ar 234 VI, its landing skids extended, drops its trolley after takeoff.

This Ar 234 B could carry 3,300 pounds of bombs and was powered by two Jumo turbojets, each delivering 1,980 pounds of thrust.

of a collapse of our air arm exists." He went on to suggest a crash program to train more pilots and to boost production of jet fighters to 1,000 a month. "At this moment, I would rather have one Me 262 than five Me 109s," he declared.

At Obersalzberg, Hitler listened with growing agitation to Galland's proposals. How many of the jets now in production carried bombs, he wanted to know. "None, my Führer," Milch confessed. "The Me 262 is being built exclusively as a fighter aircraft."

Hitler flew into a rage. "Not a single one of my orders has been obeyed," he shouted. Milch, Göring—the entire Luftwaffe—were cowards and traitors of the worst sort. Henceforth, he decreed, all Me 262s must be built as full-fledged bombers. Any reference to jet fighters, in speech or in writing, was strictly forbidden. Milch, aghast at Hitler's outburst, observed just loud enough for the Führer to overhear that "any small child could see that this is no bomber, but a fighter." Shortly afterward he was dismissed from his post. Galland had been put in a sufficiently odious light so that he too would soon fall from favor.

Luckily for Messerschmitt, the designers he had assigned to transform the Me 262 into a bomber had made substantial progress. They had fitted bomb racks to the fuselage of the plane, and the mechanism worked satisfactorily. Only minor changes were needed to make the system fully operational and these could be made during production.

As predicted by the fighter advocates, the bomber version of the Me 262 turned out to be a disappointment. The air resistance—plus the weight of a ton of explosives, a bomb sight and a release mechanism— slowed the plane so much that it could be overhauled by the Allies' fastest fighters. Though its speed increased during a bombing run, which was conducted at a shallow dive of about 30 degrees, the jet then traveled too fast for the pilot to pinpoint his target, and the bombs often fell wide of the mark. An aide pointed out this difficulty to Hitler, but the invasion that the Führer had hoped to thwart with the plane had already succeeded, and he replied: "There are so many Allied vehicles on the roads that if you drop a bomb it is sure to hit something."

Hitler scarcely exaggerated. During coming months, flying from forward bases in France, the Me 262 would achieve minor success as a bomber against Allied ground forces in central France. In July and August 1944 the pilots found that with practice they could in fact achieve the same degree of accuracy that they had when flying piston-engined fighter-bombers.

During this period, several of the Me 262s that had been built as fighters began to fly trial sorties against Allied aircraft. Based at Lechfeld, the jets had scored three kills—two P-38 Lightnings and a Mosquito— by July 25, when British Flight Lieutenant Wall encountered an Me 262 over Bavaria. General Carl Spaatz, commander of U.S. air operations in Europe, was quick to see that the plane represented a threat of unprecedented magnitude. "These deadly German fighters could make Allied bombing attacks impossible in the near future," he declared.

When Hitler learned of the Me 262's successes as a fighter, he changed his mind about it. He had begun to realize, as Albert Speer, his Minister of Armaments and War Production, wrote long after the War, that "the effect of these tiny bombers was ridiculously insignificant." Yet Hitler was reluctant to abandon the idea of the Me 262 as an attack aircraft. At the end of August he authorized the limited manufacture of jet fighters—one for every 20 Me 262 bombers. Two months later he ordered that all Me 262s coming off the assembly line from that point forward be fighters, but that each "be able to carry at least one 550-pound bomb in case of emergency." Neither Messerschmitt nor the Luftwaffe paid this demand any heed.

It was a wonder that Germany could still turn out planes at all. Aircraft factories were bombed regularly, and there were acute shortages of many raw materials, especially the nickel and chromium used to make turbine blades for jet engines. Yet manufacture of the Me 262 flourished because now the jet had first call on the limited supplies available.

Junkers moved its main turbojet plant into a network of tunnels to escape Allied bombing and began turning out Jumo 004 engines at the rate of about 300 a month, enough to match Messerschmitt's production of airplanes. Parts for the airframes were machined and assembled where such activity would be difficult to detect—in caves and forests and such innocent-looking buildings as a converted shoe factory in Bavaria. In these secret plants workers riveted aluminum panels to steel wing frames, mated stabilizers to tail fins and then trucked the components to other hidden factories for final assembly. Finished aircraft made their first runs from nearby autobahns, the four-lane superhighways Hitler had ordered built to speed the movement of goods and troops the length of Germany. Because of this resourcefulness, 101 jet fighters would be delivered to the Luftwaffe in November, 124 in December, 160 in January 1945 and 280 in February.

Meanwhile, the tactical-training squadron at Lechfeld was refining and expanding its combat operations. When its first commander, Captain Werner Thierfelder, died in a crash, the unit was turned over to one of Germany's most brilliant aces, Major Walter Nowotny. A 24-year-old Viennese of great personal charm, Nowotny in the air had the killer instincts of a falcon.

Nowi, as his pilots called him, threw himself into his new duties with characteristic zeal. He saw the Me 262 as Germany's best hope against defeat. By early autumn Kommando Nowotny, as the unit was known, had 23 jets and had been transferred to Achmer and Hesepe, airfields near the Dutch border. The Kommando stood there, athwart the approach corridor for the American bombers raiding Germany, like David against Goliath, sending up its handful of Me 262s to meet the enemy.

On the first day of combat, Kommando Nowotny lost two fighters to a technique U.S. pilots soon dubbed "rat catching," ambushing the jets as they took off or landed. Flying high above the field at Achmer, an American P-51 pilot noticed a pair of Me 262s taxiing toward the run-

Major Wolfgang Schenk, one of the Luftwaffe's top bomber pilots, established the Edelweiss Bomber Group, made up of Me 262s designed as fighters but produced as fighter-bombers on Hitler's order. Schenk's 15-plane unit, stationed near Orléans, France, in 1944, was too small to have much effect on advancing Allied troops and was pulled back to Germany for the last-ditch defense of the Reich.

Major Walter Nowotny, a leading German fighter ace with 255 kills—and one of only 27 men to win the coveted Knight's Cross with Diamonds during the War—assumed command of the first detachment of Me 262s to be used purely as fighters in July 1944. When Nowotny was shot down four months later, a saddened General Galland eulogized him as "the best young man Germany had."

way. "I waited until they were both airborne," he reported after the action, "then I headed for the attack with my flight behind me." Having just taken off, the jets were moving at less than half the Mustang's speed. The P-51 closed rapidly and opened fire on the trailing jet at 400 yards, quickly overhauling the target. "As I glanced back," the American continued, "I saw a gigantic explosion, and a sheet of red-orange flame shot out about 1,000 feet." Then the lead Me 262 was in his sights. Strikes from his machine guns knocked its canopy off, and the Me 262 rolled over into a spin and crashed. A third Me 262 was shot down that day, but only after it had bagged one of three B-24s destroyed by the jets.

While Nowi's squadron reported 19 kills in its first month at Achmer, its victories were matched one for one by Me 262 losses, many of which were due to accidents. Front-wheel struts collapsed on landing (Messerschmitt designs were notorious for fragile undercarriages) and engines caught fire when throttles were advanced too rapidly. Other planes were lost because of bomb-cratered runways and inadequate maintenance—spare parts were always in short supply and ground crews were as yet unaccustomed to the workings of the jets.

Yet once in the air with a sound plane, an Me 262 pilot had an excellent chance of a safe and successful sortie. With his plane's superior speed, he could attack so rapidly that gunners in the bombers would have a hard time keeping him in their sights. And his pass was over so quickly that the fighter escort had only seconds to react; pursuit was usually fruitless.

Nonetheless, an Me 262 pilot could on occasion find himself outmaneuvered by an Allied fighter. On November 1, Flight Sergeant Willi Banzhaff, one of Nowotny's pilots, was on a solo mission when he spotted a group of B-17s returning from a raid against synthetic-oil plants at Gelsenkirchen in the Ruhr Valley. Flying at 38,000 feet, with the bombers and their escort of Mustangs and Thunderbolts 6,000 feet or more below him, he was in a perfect position to attack. He slashed down through the umbrella of fighters, caught a P-51 in his gun sight and fired. The Mustang burst into flames. Then he headed for the bombers—and quickly found himself in trouble.

As Banzhaff leveled off behind the B-17s, a swarm of Mustangs and Thunderbolts descended on him from above. "It seemed that every American fighter plane in the sky was in a mad scramble to get in a shot at him," one Allied witness recalled. So Banzhaff resumed his dive to gain speed. At about 10,000 feet he reversed direction with a hard, climbing turn at full throttle. His intention was to outclimb and outturn his pursuers, but it was a mistake. The American fighters may not have been able to catch up, but they could cut him off as he turned. Soon Banzhaff was being hammered by .50-caliber machine-gun fire. The bullets ripped into his left wing and engine. An evasive turn put him square in the gun sight of a Thunderbolt. A shower of bullets struck his right engine, setting it afire. His plane was now uncontrollable, and Banzhaff bailed out to safety.

Predecessor of the Go 229, a Horten flying wing equipped with fixed landing gear darts through the air during a 1944 test flight.

Captured in 1945, the P 1101 was sent in its unfinished state to the U.S. Six years later, an American derivative, the Bell X-5, took to the air.

German designs that foretold the future

Desperate to create a miracle jet that might turn the tide in the waning days of the War, German engineers came up with three revolutionary planes that were startlingly ahead of their time.

The Gotha 229 flying wing was born as a glider *(left),* but its designers hoped to produce a high-speed fighter by marrying turbojets to its drag-resistant form. One flew at 497 mph in 1945 and was still being tested when the War ended. In the U.S., Northrop later built its own jet-powered flying wing. It abandoned the plane when stability problems proved too difficult to solve. Improved technology has reawakened interest in the idea.

For the Junkers 287 *(below)* the Germans chose forward-swept wings over sweptback wings to delay the onset of air compressibility and gain stability at low speeds. The craft was built in 1944, partly from sections of several other planes, including the nose wheels of a downed U.S. Consolidated B-24. The Ju 287 had made 17 test flights when Soviet troops seized it in 1945. The Soviets apparently tested the plane for three years, then scrapped it. More than 30 years later in the U.S., Grumman engineers, using the latest in structural technology, applied the principle to the X-29A.

The Messerschmitt P 1101 *(below, left),* the first jet with variable-sweep wings, was still under construction when the War ended. Although the P 1101 never flew, the concept of swing wings would find application in the American F-14 and F-111 fighters of the 1970s, the B-1 bomber of the 1980s and a whole generation of Soviet fighters.

Tufts of wool cover the fuselage and forward-swept wings of the Ju 287. The wool was attached by engineers in order to study airflow.

On November 8, a week after Banzhaff's close call, Nowotny was breakfasting with Galland, who as Luftwaffe fighter chief had come to Achmer to see how the squadron's performance might be improved. A klaxon interrupted the meal, scrambling the pilots to intercept a stream of B-17s invisible above an overcast, heading into Germany.

Nowotny rose and headed for his plane, but Galland stopped him. "I need you here at headquarters to coordinate the missions," he said. "You can't fly today." Biting back his disappointment, Nowi returned to the operations room to follow the battle by radio.

The first flight of jets took off, and then the second. The bark of 30-millimeter cannon cut through the overcast, mixing with the thud of flak and the chatter of American machine guns. A few minutes later casualty reports started coming in. One jet had crash-landed. Another had stopped transmitting—a sign that it, too, had probably been hit.

Nowi could stand it no longer. "General, I am going to fly," he announced. And before Galland could stop him, he was at the wheel of his staff car, racing across the bomb-cratered airfield toward his Me 262. A few minutes later he was airborne and climbing steeply.

Nowotny's voice cut through the static on the operations room radio, ordering an attack on the nearest bomber group. He reported a kill, and large chunks of a B-17 rained down on the airfield. Two more victories quickly followed, then trouble. "I've been hit," radioed Nowotny.

Galland and the others in the operations room ran out onto the field. A crippled Me 262 could be seen plunging earthward through a break in

A Gloster Meteor nudges out of control a V-1 carrying 1,874 pounds of explosives.

Knocking down buzz bombs with Meteors

After four years of development, seven Gloster Meteors—Britain's first jet fighters—joined the RAF in July 1944 to help intercept German V-1 buzz bombs hurtling daily toward London at 300 to 400 mph. Capable of speeds up to 490 mph, the Meteors could outfly the missiles but could not shoot them down easily because of faulty guns.

When Meteor pilot T. D. Dean targeted a V-1 on August 4th, his 20-mm. cannon jammed. He nonetheless secured the first combat victory for an Allied jet by maneuvering alongside the missile, sliding a wing tip beneath a bomb wing and then banking sharply to unbalance the V-1 and send it crashing to earth.

the clouds, trailed by a pair of Mustangs. A white mushroom of cloth puffed out through the cockpit canopy—a partially opened parachute. Then the jet nosed down sharply into a steep dive, dropping like an artillery shell, the parachute still attached. There was a high-pitched whistle, followed by an explosion as the airplane hit the ground.

A pillar of thick, oily smoke guided the rescue party to the crash site. As the rescuers poked through the debris of hot, twisted metal, they uncovered a charred, severed hand, and nearby a piece of the Knight's Cross with Diamonds. That was all that remained of Major Nowotny.

With Nowotny's death, the Kommando at Achmer was dismantled and the few pilots left returned to Lechfeld. During its period of operation, it had lost 26 aircraft but had discovered some vital truths about the handling and deployment of Me 262s—lessons that were quickly put to use by the nucleus of a new jet-fighter group, Jagdgeschwader 7. Fresh pilots, instead of being sent aloft in a Me 262 with only a cursory briefing on the idiosyncracies of the aircraft, were now to receive 35 hours of flight training. That was still not enough and few pilots actually got even that many hours. But it was infinitely better than the way Kommando Nowotny had been sent into combat.

As Jagdgeschwader 7 grew, it systematically refined its tactics. One result was that jet units abandoned the Luftwaffe's standard attack formation of four aircraft, called a *Schwarm,* or swarm. This arrangement consisted of a pair of two-plane elements, each with a leader and a wingman. While one element led, the second covered from behind at a slightly higher altitude. Maintaining this formation required continual speed adjustments. Because the Jumo 004 engine often flamed out at combat altitudes when throttle settings were rapidly changed, such shifts in speed were very risky. So, instead, the jets adopted a looser, three-plane V formation that did not require as much attention to the throttles. The tactic made it more difficult for the planes to watch out for one another in a battle, but the jets, with their ability to outrun virtually any enemy fighter, could usually take care of themselves.

Jagdgeschwader 7 found that the tactic used by the Luftwaffe's piston-engined fighters against bombers—a head-on assault to concentrate fire on the bombers' vulnerable glassed-in noses—was of little use. The closing speed of the jets was more than 800 miles per hour, giving the pilots only a few seconds to aim and fire. So Me 262 pilots struck from the rear, in trios, with the jets spaced 150 yards apart. From about three miles behind, and a mile higher than the bombers, the Me 262s would "bounce" a formation, stabbing downward through the fighter escort at 500 miles per hour or more. The pilots soon discovered that by dropping about 500 yards below their targets, then pulling up to cut the closing speed to 300 miles per hour, they could climb through the bomber formation and spray the underbellies and tail sections of the Fortresses and Liberators with cannon shells as they went. They would then exit through the top of the formation. Staying beneath the bombers was deemed suicidal; flaming debris could easily damage or even bring down a jet. The attack completed, the Me 262s would circle and repeat the maneuver or, if low on fuel, dash for home.

With such tactics, Jagdgeschwader 7 squadrons, dispersed to various German airfields, began scoring an impressive number of victories. Jagdgeschwader 7's Wing 3, with only 30 planes in service on any one day, was shooting down Allied aircraft at the rate of about 100 a month; it would claim 427 kills before the War's end, though Allied analysis of the battles later disputed this score.

On March 18, 1945, thirty-seven Me 262s scrambled against 1,200 Flying Fortresses that were being escorted to Berlin by more than 600 fighters—one of the largest aerial armadas in history. Outnumbered nearly 50 to 1, the jets managed to down eight bombers and one fighter. The victories were tempered by the loss of four Me 262s, more than 10 per cent of those sent aloft.

During this action a new weapon even more devastating than the Messerschmitt's 30-millimeter cannon was used for the first time. It was the R4M rocket *(page 30)*. Each fighter carried 24 of the missiles, a number calculated to give a bomber no chance to survive. On April 4, Lieutenant Fritz Mueller intercepted a formation of Liberators. "I fired off all my rockets," he recalled after the battle. "They struck the fuselage and wing of one of the Liberators flying in the middle of the formation. It reared up, fell back, then began to go down."

Yet by now, the jet, the weapons, the victories hardly mattered. For all its unquestioned superiority, there was not much that the Me 262 could accomplish against the overwhelming weight of Allied air power. In the end, it became little more than a talisman of shattered hopes and defiant pride as the noose tightened around what remained of Hitler's Reich. The armies of Great Britain and the United States had already crossed the Rhine and were rumbling through the farmlands and cities of western Germany. The Russians had swept across the Oder and were pressing toward the outskirts of Berlin.

Nevertheless, as the War rolled toward its finish, the Me 262 continued to fly. Of all the jet units, none experienced such a brief, bright flash of glory as Jagdverband 44. This fighter squadron went into action in April 1945, just a month before the German surrender. Its 50 pilots were battlewise veterans—their combined kills in piston-engined fighters added up to more than 1,000. Colonel Johannes Steinhoff, for example, had 170 kills; Lieutenant Colonel Heinz Baer, 204. No fewer than 10 of the pilots wore the Knight's Cross. Their leader, fittingly, was the Luftwaffe's staunchest champion of jet fighters, General Galland.

The preceding January, Galland had been relieved of command of the Luftwaffe's fighters; he had been on the wrong side of Hitler and Göring on too many issues. To keep him busy and out of everyone's way, Galland had been given a free hand to form his own frontline command. That suited the general just fine. He combed through squadron rosters for the best pilots in the Luftwaffe and even rounded up old flying buddies who had been wounded in action and were still recover-

In an unorthodox arrangement that saved manufacturing time, the Heinkel 162 Volksjaeger (People's Fighter) carries its single jet engine atop the fuselage. Designed and assembled in just 73 days at the close of 1944, the prototype had wooden wings, tail fins and nose cap. Though 275 such fighters were built, none were ready for combat by War's end.

ing in hospital wards. He led them through a lightning-fast training course in jets at Brandenburg-Briest airfield outside Berlin. Neither Galland nor his men thought their unit could influence the War. "The magic word 'jet' had brought us together," Galland explained later. "We wanted to be known as the last fighter pilots of the Luftwaffe."

Deployed at Riem, near Munich, Jagdverband 44 was troubled by all the shortages that had become routine in the Reich—lack of planes, parts and fuel; shoddy maintenance; and an airfield that was under almost continuous Allied attack. Yet the pilots were possessed by a kind of fighting frenzy. "We could do nothing but fly and fight and do our duty as fighter pilots to the last," Galland recalled. And as the veterans sortied into combat, their kills mounted. Pilot after pilot won his laurels as a jet ace, with five or more kills. Lieutenant Colonel Baer scored 16 victories in the final weeks of the War to run his total to 220.

But the moment quickly passed. Allied planes were pounding the Riem airstrip regularly, blasting new craters in the runway almost as fast as workers, hundreds of them, filled in the holes. The jets were dispersed around the field and well camouflaged, but "bringing the aircraft onto the field and taking off became more and more difficult," Galland remembered. "Eventually it was a matter of luck." And all the while, Allied ground troops pushed closer, threatening to engulf the field.

On April 26, Galland led six Me 262s against a flight of B-26 Marauders heading south toward Munich. Galland approached the twin-engined medium bombers from the front, passing over them and then turning back; he would attack from the rear, in the prescribed manner.

Galland released the safety on his rockets and 30-millimeter cannon as the enemy's tail guns began to blink balefully. Tense and excited as usual in combat, he lined up his rockets on the rearmost Marauder. "I was in the best firing position," he said later; "I had aimed accurately and pressed my thumb flat on the release button—with no result. Maddening!'' He had forgotten about a second safety on the missiles.

It was a careless lapse, but not irremediable. His cannon were working, and as he blasted away he watched the bomber explode. A second or two later he had swept to the head of the formation and was pumping cannon shells into one of the raiders in the lead. It seemed like a sure kill, and he banked steeply to the left to see if the bomber would go down.

That was Galland's second mistake. Unnoticed in the heat of action, a flight of Thunderbolts had been assessing the battle from high overhead. Now they fell upon the vulnerable jet. "A hail of fire enveloped me," Galland remembered. "A sharp rap hit my right knee. The instrument panel was shattered. The right engine was also hit. Its metal covering worked loose in the wind and was partly carried away. Now the left engine was hit too. I could hardly hold her in the air."

Galland repressed an intense urge to bail out, worried that he would be shot while descending in his parachute. Finding that he could exert a measure of control over his crippled fighter, he turned toward Riem, trailing smoke. Galland was over the field in less than a minute, but on starting his approach he discovered that one engine could not be throttled back. So to lose speed he cut off the fuel to both engines, and coasted toward a dead-stick landing. Only then did he realize that the field was being strafed by Thunderbolts. But with his engines dead, Galland had no choice but to touch down on the runway. An eternity seemed to pass before the brakes hauled the plane to a stop; then Galland leaped from the cockpit and into the relative security of the nearest bomb crater.

It was Galland's last mission; bullet shards in his knee sent him off to the hospital in Munich. But Jagdverband 44, retreating eastward to Salzburg, Austria, kept fighting for another week, until American tanks clanked onto the airfield. During its brief life the unit had scored 50 kills.

And so the Allies took over, one by one, the last sanctuaries of the world's first fighting jet. Some planes were captured on the ground; some were found burning, splashed with gasoline and set on fire by their pilots. And some were discovered weeks after the fighting had ended, in the forest clearings of Bavaria, as though awaiting delivery to Luftwaffe ghost squadrons. Somehow they seemed like curious afterthoughts, both poignant and faintly ominous, a bright new miracle weapon that had arrived too late. Most Allied ground troops knew nothing of the jets. Seeing them there, abandoned in the forest, few could have realized that the planes were heralds of a new age in weaponry.

One American who shared in this innocence was the economist John Kenneth Galbraith, who traveled through Germany with the occupation forces to assess the effects of the Allied bombings on German industry. Galbraith came upon a stretch of autobahn that had been converted into an airstrip. "In cul-de-sacs along the road were curious aircraft," he reported, "sleek and without propellers. One wondered if they had been delivered without them."

An American military official inspects the wreckage inside an Me 262 plant targeted by Allied bombers shortly before the War ended.

2

A proving ground in MiG Alley

Bone-tired and pale with worry, a crowd of bewildered Westerners milled about the terminal at Kimpo Airfield, near Seoul, capital of the Republic of South Korea. They had been gathering since before first light—Army wives and children, embassy families, a few missionaries and businessmen. From the north, a dozen miles away, could be heard the rumble of artillery.

It had all happened so quickly. Just two days earlier, on June 25, 1950—at 4 o'clock of a Sunday morning—the armies of Communist North Korea had attacked along the 200-mile border between the two countries. The Communists had struck without warning, 90,000 strong, in an assault so fierce that it sent the South Korean troops reeling.

The refugees at Kimpo were increasingly apprehensive as they waited to board U.S. Air Force transports, C-47s and C-54s, that would carry them to Japan. But the evacuation was agonizingly slow. No sooner would a planeload take off than more people would show up.

Kimpo had been bombed on the first day of the War and at any moment it might be hit again. During that strike a pair of North Korean Yak-9s, prop-driven fighters built in the Soviet Union, had strafed the field, wrecking the control tower, crippling a U.S. C-54 parked on the apron and turning a nearby fuel dump into a fireball. Four other Yaks had roared down on an adjacent field used by South Korea's tiny Air Force, which consisted only of trainers. Seven of them were damaged.

American fighters of the Fifth Air Force, sent from bases in Japan, now patrolled overhead. At about 10,000 feet orbited a handful of F-82 Twin Mustangs, the last piston-engined fighters to be acquired by the U.S. Air Force. Several thousand feet above the F-82s circled four F-80 Shooting Stars, the first U.S. jet fighters to be sent into combat.

Around noon five Yaks flew in low over Seoul and, either failing to see the F-82s or ignoring them, nosed down in a long, slanting dive toward Kimpo. The F-82s pounced, and the result was a rout. In a whirling dogfight that lasted less than five minutes, the Americans shot down three Yaks and drove off the other two.

Then about an hour later the North Koreans tried again. Eight Il-10 Shturmoviks, piston-engined ground-attack fighters of Russian origin, were droning toward Kimpo when they were met by four Shooting Stars. One devastating pass was all the Americans needed. Captain Raymond Schillereff lined up a Shturmovik in his sights, fired a burst from his .50-caliber machine guns and watched the enemy spiral into a

Through an Oriental-style gateway proclaiming their North Korean destination, two U.S. pilots walk toward their F-86 Sabre jets parked on Kimpo Airfield near Seoul. Named for the Russian-built fighters that haunted it, MiG Alley lay athwart the North Korean-Chinese border, and was the scene of the jet age's first large-scale air battles.

rice paddy. Behind him, Lieutenant Robert Wayne scored the second kill and then a third. Lieutenant Robert Dewald knocked out a fourth. The remaining Shturmoviks turned tail, leaving the Kimpo airlift to proceed unmolested. It was the first time American jets had fired their guns in earnest, and they had netted four kills as easily as mowing grass.

Within days of the invasion, the United Nations Security Council called upon members of the world body for troops to drive the aggressor back above the 38th Parallel, the boundary between North and South Korea. President Harry Truman ordered his Far East commander in Tokyo, General Douglas MacArthur, to join the battle. To help with the job he sent the aircraft carrier *Valley Forge* as the nucleus of an international naval task force. Great Britain contributed the Royal Navy's carrier *Triumph.* "We've got to stop those sons of bitches no matter what," Truman declared. No one doubted that the "police action," as the U.N. response was being called, would succeed—and quickly. "When the Fifth Air Force gets to work," growled one senior U.S. Air Force officer, "there won't be a North Korean left in the Republic."

But it was not to be. The War would drag on for three dismal years, raging up and down the Korean peninsula as the Communists poured in a seemingly inexhaustible supply of manpower. Troops of 16 member nations—from the United States and Canada to Australia and Thailand—would be involved, but their numbers never would be enough to match the enemy's. And while the infantry slugged it out in the mud, another battle would be fought to gain control of the skies, with pilots of both sides locked in history's first aerial duels between jet aircraft.

The U.S. was a relative latecomer to jets. Its earliest jet plane, Bell Aircraft Corporation's twin-engined XP-59 Airacomet, did not take to the air until September 1942, well after Germany's Messerschmitt 262 in Germany and England's Gloster Meteor. Developed in secrecy— dummy propellers confounded foreign agents—the XP-59 proved to be a disappointment. With a top speed of only 413 miles per hour, the plane was no faster than the Air Forces' prop-driven fighters.

About nine months after the XP-59's unveiling, Lockheed Aircraft Corporation began work on a jet. After 143 days of concentrated effort, the company came up in January 1944 with the single-engined F-80 Shooting Star, which could streak along easily at 560 miles per hour. One souped-up model would reach 623.8 miles per hour, a record.

The Shooting Star turned out to be a plane of remarkable versatility. With six .50-caliber machine guns mounted in the nose, and racks on the wings for 16 armor-piercing rockets and a pair of 1,000-pound bombs or 265-gallon drop tanks, the jet could be put to any number of tasks—as a pure fighter, as an escort for heavy bombers or as a ground-attack plane. The Air Force eventually took delivery of 2,000 of them.

Sixteen months after the first F-80 came off the production line, the Republic Aviation Company unveiled a second U.S. jet fighter, the powerful F-84 Thunderjet. Designed from the start as a fighter-bomber,

An F2H-2 Banshee snags an arresting cable on the flight deck of the U.S.S. Essex after completing a mission. With a top speed of only 582 mph, the Navy jet was no match for the faster MiG-15 in the dogfights over the Yalu River; it was used primarily as a fighter-bomber and for fleet protection off the Korean coast.

the Thunderjet models used in Korea had a range of nearly 2,000 miles—long legs for a jet of that era—which made it suitable for escorting bombers. Grumman Aircraft Engineering Corporation weighed in almost two years later with the F9F Panther, a fighter-bomber for the Navy's aircraft carriers. The Panther carried four 20-millimeter cannon in the nose and six 5-inch rockets or two 500-pound bombs under the wings. Tanks on the wing tips gave the plane a range of 1,350 miles.

The Shooting Star, the Thunderjet and the Panther were more than adequate to meet the challenge of the North Korean Air Force in the early months of the War. During the two days that followed their ill-fated raids on Kimpo, the Yaks and Shturmoviks, seemingly cowed by the Fifth Air Force, huddled on their fields, the chief of which was at Pyongyang, the North Korean capital. When U.S. reconnaissance photographs showed more than 100 fighters parked there, U.S. and British planes were sent on July 3 to wipe them out and crater the runway.

The attack proceeded according to plan. Propeller-driven Corsairs and Skyraiders were catapulted from the deck of the *Valley Forge*. British piston-engined Seafires and Fireflies took off from the *Triumph*. A short time later, two squadrons of faster F9F Panther jets roared into the air from the *Valley Forge* to rendezvous with the prop planes as they approached the target. The Panthers' task was to neutralize any defense that the Yaks might put up.

When the Panthers arrived, North Korean pilots scrambled to ward off the attack. Several Yaks rose into the air, but one that was just taking off caught the eye of Lieutenant (jg.) Leonard Plog. "I banked over to my right and pulled up behind him," Plog recalled. "By the time I got into firing position he was well airborne, about 350 feet in the air."

As Plog closed in, tracers from the 20-millimeter cannon of a second

Yak flashed past his left shoulder. "That dirty S.O.B. is trying to kill me," Plog thought. He hauled back on the stick and watched the tracers fall below him. At the same moment, Plog's wingman, Ensign E. W. Brown, moved in from behind and caught the Yak in his gun sight. "The next thing I saw," Plog remembered, "was a terrific explosion and Yak parts flying around." It was the first kill by a Navy jet.

Plog then turned back to his own quarry, which was still straining for altitude up ahead. "I got a couple of lucky hits on his starboard wing and it just peeled away," he recalled. "The Yak flipped over and crashed." Now, with little or nothing to fear from enemy planes, Plog and Brown, joined by other Panthers, began strafing the airfield, hitting 10 aircraft, the control tower and some fire engines, setting a small fuel dump afire. Then they headed back to the *Valley Forge.* The next day the Panthers returned with the Corsairs and Skyraiders to blast the field again.

These and successive raids reduced the North Korean Air Force from about 130 warplanes to scarcely 18 operable aircraft. Panthers and Air Force Shooting Stars could now turn their full attention to the support of hard-pressed U.N. foot soldiers. The hordes of North Koreans seemed unstoppable. "They struck like a cobra," declared General MacArthur, and within five weeks they had pushed 250 miles southward. All that was left to the defenders was a mere toe hold of ground, about 75 miles across, surrounding the port of Pusan in the southeast. Here Mac-Arthur's troops dug in, lent just enough strength by American air power to hold the perimeter, yet too weak to break out.

Shooting Stars flew in from Japan to attack North Korean positions. It was dangerous, unrelenting work, with scores of guns firing back, and it offered little glory. But the bombs, rockets and machine-gun bullets the jets rained down prevented the North Koreans from massing for an all-out assault on the Pusan perimeter. One of the F-80s' most effective weapons was a jellied gasoline called napalm. Carried in a pair of 110-pound canisters suspended from bomb pylons under the wings, napalm splashed a wide area when it hit, engulfing whatever it touched in a 2,000° F. cascade of flame.

Rockets and napalm might keep 70,000 North Korean troops encircling Pusan tied down, but these weapons could not dislodge them. A bold new strategy was needed, and it came from MacArthur. He proposed a seaborne assault on the port of Inchon, 20 miles west of Seoul and far behind enemy lines. By surprising the Communists from the rear, he hoped to recapture Seoul, South Korea's rail and road center, and cut off supplies to North Korean forces in the South. The operation posed substantial risk, but MacArthur was convinced the landing would succeed. "I can almost hear the ticking of the second hand of destiny," he told a skeptical General J. Lawton Collins, the Army Chief of Staff, at a conference in Tokyo. "We must act now or we will die. We shall land at Inchon and I shall crush them."

On September 15, troops of the 1st Marine Division clambered up Inchon's 12-foot sea walls and secured two beachheads. The landing cost the lives of just 20 Americans. Two days later, after driving 10 miles north, the Marines recaptured Kimpo Airfield. Twelve days after swarming ashore, they entered Seoul and unfurled the blue-and-white banner of the U.N. from the dome of the capitol.

Now MacArthur moved to relieve the besieged U.N. troops at Pusan. On September 17, Fifth Air Force Shooting Stars and Mustangs began a series of murderous strikes along the perimeter, enveloping the North Koreans in a flaming tide of napalm. That night formations of B-29 heavy bombers from Japan and Okinawa unrolled a carpet of 500-pound bombs, and two days later the embattled troops broke through the perimeter. The Communists, isolated by the landing to the north, bolted as the U.N. ground forces began to advance. Hundreds of Communist troops milled about aimlessly in the open or streamed northward along roads where they were easy targets for roving F-80s and other fighter-bombers. On September 21, for example, almost half of a force of 30 enemy tanks was destroyed by Shooting Stars and Mustangs. At the end of a week, the North Korean Army was all but defeated, and on

An F-80 Shooting Star drops a pod-shaped napalm canister onto a North Korean storage depot as antiaircraft fire, marked by a faint trail of smoke, rises diagonally from a gun emplacement at the bend in the road. During this May 1952 raid on Suan, a supply center southeast of the capital of Pyongyang, more than 12,000 gallons of napalm were released over a two-square-mile area.

September 29, General MacArthur and South Korea's President, Syngman Rhee, marched through Seoul in a victory parade.

With South Korea won, MacArthur cast his eye beyond the 38th Parallel. No formal plans had been laid to follow the enemy into North Korea; it just seemed to happen. U.N. forces, in hot pursuit of the retreating North Koreans, swept past Pyongyang, 120 miles north of Seoul, and on toward the Yalu River, the boundary between North Korea and the Chinese province of Manchuria. As the infantry advanced, the U.S. Air Force began to rebuild and enlarge South Korean airfields. Three squadrons of F-80s were transferred from Japan to Kimpo, and three others to a strip at Taegu farther south. Two squadrons of Royal Australian Air Force Meteors set up base at Pusan.

The very scope of the U.N. victories carried an implicit risk: The closer MacArthur's forces moved to the Chinese border, the greater the possibility that Asia's largest Communist power might intervene in the fighting. The Chinese Premier, Chou En-lai, had already issued warnings to the U.N. that any further advances into North Korea would bring his country into the battle.

Chou was not bluffing. On October 19, troops of the People's Republic of China began crossing the Yalu under cover of stormy weather. Six days later, they attacked, all 180,000 of them. One division struck at Sudong in the central highlands. Another encircled part of South Korea's 3rd Division in the west, annihilating two full regiments. The Chinese thrust southward and on November 1 smashed past Sinuiju on the south bank of the Yalu, forcing the U.S. 21st Infantry to retreat. And that same day, as a flight of F-51 Mustangs patrolled the Yalu, six sweptwing aircraft bearing the red star of the Chinese Air Force flashed out of the sky, their stubby silver fuselages streaking past at near-supersonic speed. They were Russian-built MiG-15s, the first Communist jet fighters to see combat. Alert flying by the Mustang pilots—and the poor marksmanship of the MiG pilots—allowed the F-51s to escape unscathed. An entirely new air war had begun.

The MiG-15 had been conceived in the demise of Hitler's Reich. No other power had compiled such a wealth of data on high-speed-jet technology as Germany, and the victorious Allies would make wide use of this fund of knowledge. The Soviet Union, moving in from the East, captured several German aircraft factories and their resident technicians, designers and some production-line jet fighters—including Willy Messerschmitt's Me 262. Studying this pioneering craft, Russian engineers quickly fixed upon its most revolutionary feature—the swept wings that brought it to the edge of supersonic flight. Two leading aircraft designers, Artem Mikoyan and Mikhail Gurevich, were already at work on a Soviet jet fighter, and they borrowed from—and improved upon—Messerschmitt's sweptwing design. For their engine, they used a direct copy of a Rolls-Royce turbojet purchased in England after it was released for export in 1947 by the British Labor government.

During the Korean War, the Communist MiG pilots had the advantage of operating close to their home bases, while the American Sabre pilots based in South Korea had to fly a couple of hundred miles in order to join the battle. This map shows the principal North Korean (red stars) and United Nations (black stars) air bases; the shaded area, where most of the combat took place, was known as MiG Alley.

The result was the MiG-15. Its public debut, on Soviet Aviation Day, 1948, alarmed military analysts in the West. They had had no idea that the Russians had progressed so far, so quickly.

The U.S. had captured some Me 262s as well, and also a massive archive of Luftwaffe technical files. And here too, in page after page of wind-tunnel test results, the sweptwing design showed its high-speed superiority. Designers at North American Aviation Company, builder of the exemplary Mustang of World War II, saw in this research the answer to performance problems they were having with a new single-engined jet fighter being developed for the Air Force. They redesigned the craft's wings to angle them back 35 degrees. From their efforts eventually emerged the F-86 Sabre, America's first sweptwing jet.

Whistling along at 675 miles per hour, the F-86 shattered all speed records. It was both highly maneuverable and rock steady in the air—an ideal platform for aiming and firing its six .50-caliber machine guns in the nose. The controls were so responsive, declared one pilot, "that they seemed actuated by thought." It was the only Western fighter that came near to matching Russia's MiG-15. Indeed, both planes, with their angled-back wings, their compact stub-nosed bodies and their forward-mounted cockpit canopies, were remarkably alike in both looks and performance. Only in rate of climb and service ceiling did the MiG outstrip the Sabre. And so slight was the difference in profile—the MiG had a somewhat shorter body and a larger tail with the stabilizer mounted well above the fuselage—that pilots, when the two planes finally met in combat over Korea, had trouble telling them apart.

At the outbreak of the War, there was no thought of sending the three U.S.-based Sabre groups to Korea; the air war was being fought handily enough by the Shooting Stars and F-51 Mustangs based in Japan, aided by Navy Panthers from the carrier task force in the Yellow Sea.

The scenario changed when the first Chinese MiG-15s screamed across the Yalu and all too soon tangled with the F-80s. On November 8, a fleet of 70 B-29s had set out to strike Sinuiju. Not only did the city serve as the temporary seat of the North Korean government, but linked to China by two bridges, it was the main funnel for supplies and munitions flowing in from Manchuria. Some of the B-29s were supposed to knock down the spans with high-explosive bombs; others were assigned to torch the city with incendiaries. And running interference for the bombers, advance squadrons of F-51s and F-80 fighter-bombers were to soften up the antiaircraft batteries with napalm and rockets.

As the B-29s dropped bombs through the smoke of burning gun emplacements, an escort of Shooting Stars circled watchfully at 20,000 feet. Six MiGs rose from Antung, climbed to 30,000 feet and then, in pairs, dived on the U.S. jets. The F-80s turned to meet them, throwing the MiGs into confusion. The Chinese jets loosed a wildly inaccurate shower of cannon fire at the F-80s, then zoomed out of combat—except for one. Its pilot chose to dive away, and that was a mistake.

The cratered runway of a North Korean air base shows the damage inflicted by B-29s during a night raid. Most of the 20 MiG-15s in curved revetments

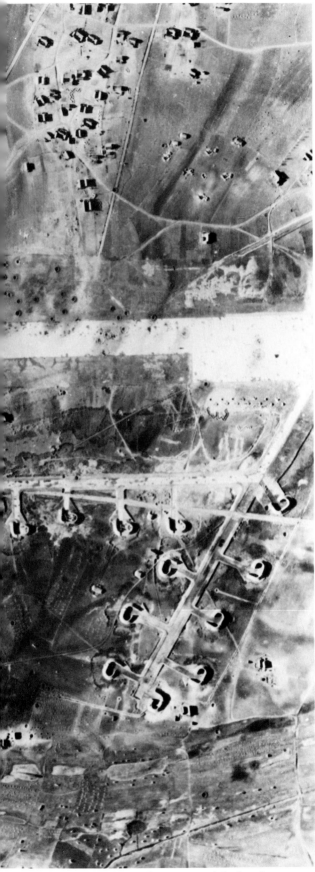

along the taxiway seem to have escaped the bombs.

Lieutenant Russell Brown nosed down in pursuit; in a descent the F-80, being heavier than the MiG, had a slight speed advantage. Brown narrowed the distance, squeezed the trigger on his control stick and sent a five-second burst of .50-caliber fire into the enemy plane. The MiG spiraled earthward, trailing white smoke, and crashed into the river-bank. The world's first encounter between jet fighters had lasted perhaps 30 seconds, and it had ended in an American victory.

The B-29s, meanwhile, had unleashed a minor holocaust on Sinuiju, burning down 60 per cent of the city with huge tonnages of incendiaries. But somehow the two vital bridges remained standing. Two days later a second strike was called, and then a third. Still the bridges refused to drop. And as the raids continued, both at Sinuiju and at other trans-Yalu links to the east, the more aggressive MiGs managed to cut through the Shooting Star escorts and bring down or damage four bombers in as many raids. The MiGs had to be neutralized, so the U.S. Air Force decided to send Sabres to Korea. On December 13, 1950, F-86s of the 4th Fighter-Interceptor Wing arrived at Kimpo, primed for action. Their mission: to patrol the 100-mile-wide strip of airspace below the Yalu, already becoming known as MiG Alley, thereby preventing MiGs from dashing out of China and attacking U.N. bombers.

A blizzard and its messy aftermath grounded the Sabres for three days. On December 17, the sky cleared, and shortly after 2 o'clock in the afternoon four planes, designated Baker Flight, lifted off. As they headed north toward MiG Alley, the four planes took up the standard U.S. Air Force attack formation—the so-called finger four, for its resemblance to the extended fingertips of an open hand. This arrangement, with four sharp-eyed pilots on the lookout for MiGs, offered the craft mutual security against surprise attack. But once enemy planes were sighted and the action was under way, the finger four would normally split into two elements for greater maneuverability. Each consisted of a leader and a wingman. The wingman's job was to stick with his leader as he pressed the attack, and to warn him if an enemy threatened to come in at 6 o'clock, as the sector directly aft of a fighter's vulnerable tail is known.

Lieutenant Colonel Bruce Hinton, commander of the 336th Fighter-Interceptor Squadron, led Baker Flight that day. According to a plan formulated at higher echelon, Hinton held the speed to a leisurely 400 miles per hour or so, both to conserve fuel and as a ruse: It was hoped that Chinese radar operators would mistake the F-86s for the slower Shooting Stars and would send MiGs rushing to the attack. The masquerade worked, for as the Sabres neared Antung and turned east along the Yalu, Hinton heard his wingman's voice over the radio: "Baker Lead, I have bogies at 9 o'clock low and crossing."

Four MiGs had taken off from Antung. They were about a mile ahead and climbing at full power toward the plodding Sabres. "It was a completely startling sight," he remembered; "their speed was astonishing!"

Hinton punched his mike button. "Baker Flight, drop tanks," he ordered; relieved of the weight and drag of their auxiliary fuel tanks, the Sabres would be able to fly at top speed. Hinton listened for the expected acknowledgment, but none came. There could be only one explanation—his transmitter had gone dead.

Hinton tried the radio switches once or twice, then returned his attention to the approaching MiGs. They crossed in front of him, and banked right to come around from behind. "No time to lose," thought Hinton. "I punched off the tanks. A hard pull into their turn brought me in at their 5 o'clock and closing."

Now above and behind the MiGs, Hinton was in perfect position to attack. He checked his Machmeter, an instrument that tells how fast a plane is flying in comparison with the speed of sound. The pointer had edged past Mach .95; Hinton was nudging the sound barrier and had exceeded his aircraft's red line, its theoretical safe speed limit. His closest target was the MiG leader's wingman. At 1,500 feet, he let go a burst of bullets that splashed and twinkled behind the enemy's cockpit and out across his right wing. Then a chilling thought raced through his mind. Could the MiG leader, who had climbed 200 feet and had fallen back nearly abreast of Hinton, position himself to hit him or his wingman?

His wingman! Hinton scanned the sky but could not see him. Then he realized what had happened. While he was fiddling with his transmitter, the rest of his flight had somehow drifted off. Hinton was now alone, and the MiG leader seemed to be angling over to attack. Still, Hinton wanted to finish off the crippled jet in front of him.

The MiG pilot was making all kinds of mistakes. He extended his speed brakes, then quickly retracted them, but the momentary drag only served to put the Sabre squarely on his tail. Hinton bucked and twisted a moment in the MiG's jet wash, slid to one side and, from a distance of 800 feet, sent a long burst of machine-gun fire into the tailpipe. Pieces of engine flew out, along with a geyser of flame. But the MiG continued flying. Hinton moved in for a closer look.

"We hung there in the sky, turning left," he remembered, "with my airplane tight against his underside in a slow formation. We were about five feet apart and I got a good close look at his MiG. It was beautiful, a sports car of a fighter." And still it would not fall. "Why doesn't he blow?" Hinton wondered. He hammered the faltering MiG with bullets until, finally, it flipped onto its back and plummeted earthward.

Hinton saw no other MiGs, so he set course for Kimpo. Arriving 20 minutes later, he streaked low over the runway at more than 500 miles per hour and executed the traditional victory roll.

As the Sabres began making regular sorties into MiG Alley, a new set of tactics was developed. The slow cruising speed used by Hinton put the jets at a disadvantage, since the MiGs almost always attacked at near-maximum velocity. So the 4th Wing started flying faster as it entered the combat area. But the higher throttle setting used more fuel and reduced patrol time along the Yalu from 35 minutes or so to 20 minutes. The solution was to schedule flights into MiG Alley at five-minute intervals. With the staggered flights, there were enough F-86s to maintain a 60-minute shield behind which U.N. bombers could operate.

The revised tactics brought a dramatic victory on December 22, when two Sabre flights engaged a force of 16 MiGs in a swirling dogfight lasting nearly 20 minutes. The contending jets chased one another in high-speed turning duels, spiraling downward from 30,000 feet to the treetops and then zooming again. One Sabre pilot was caught in a turn and shot down, but his comrades quickly dispatched six MiGs.

These early encounters at jet speed put harsh new stresses on a fighter pilot. Below him, as the president of North American once put it, was "a giant blowtorch delivering as much effective power as three large Diesel locomotives." Swooping and turning high above the clouds, with the horizon dissolving into haze, he had to be doubly alert. Two jets heading straight for each other could close at a rate exceeding 20 miles per minute. At such speeds, a pilot had only a few seconds to react and get the upper hand in an encounter.

Performing combat maneuvers at speeds greater than 600 miles per hour could impose crushing G-forces that would push a pilot deep into his seat. These forces made it difficult to fire a jet's guns accurately in a sharp turn, and it was rare for a flier to line up directly behind his wildly evading target for an easy shot. Moreover, G-forces deprive a pilot's brain of blood, thus threatening to bring on unconsciousness. American pilots wore G-suits that countered this hazard, but the Communists did not. Time and again a Sabre would engage a MiG in a turning duel only to see the enemy enter a spin and crash; the pilot may have simply blacked out. Or, because the MiG-15 tended to become unstable at high speeds, he may have lost control of his aircraft. Even when flying straight and level near the red line, the Russian jet would oscillate, swinging from side to side and making it difficult for the pilot to hold his guns on his adversary.

By the end of December the Sabres had run up a spectacular kill ratio of 8 to 1. But success would soon be interrupted, not by any response from the Chinese Air Force, but because the war on the ground had again taken a dismal turn. The Chinese, after their initial offensive, had paused to build up their strength, and in late November had attacked again. They smashed through the U.N. positions in overwhelming force. There seemed to be no stopping them. "It was like throwing pebbles at rollers in surf," said one battle-weary U.S. Marine. "They didn't care if they were killed." The Chinese recaptured Pyongyang, then Seoul and its vital jet airfield at Kimpo, pushing the Sabres back to Japan just weeks after they had come to Korea. Because of the distances now involved, patrols in MiG Alley had to be abandoned. By late January, the Communists had forged 70 miles into South Korea. There the U.N. forces rallied, held and then began to drive north once again. On March 14, they took Seoul, and the 4th Wing could return to battle.

But Kimpo was thought too close to the enemy for the Sabres' safety, so they resumed their patrols from Suwon, about 20 miles south of Seoul.

Facilities at the airstrip were primitive at best. Winterized tents served for sleeping as well as working. Perforated steel plates laid down on the sea of mud flanking the airstrip made a serviceable parking and maintenance area. But when the mud dried, it turned to dust that was sucked into the engines, shortening their life.

Perhaps the base's worst feature was the 4,900-foot runway. It was barely long enough for the F-86s, and there was no taxi strip beside it. Pilots who had just landed taxied back to the parking area along the runway's left side while other pilots touched down virtually head on at 120 miles per hour on the opposite side. This hair-raising practice continued for almost six months before the runway was lengthened and a taxi strip constructed.

Among the pilots stationed at Suwon was Captain James Jabara. A veteran Mustang pilot from World War II, he shot down four MiGs in little more than a month. Then his unit, the 334th Fighter-Interceptor Squadron, was ordered back to Japan in a scheduled rotation of forces. Jabara was dismayed. He needed only one victory more to become an ace, the first in Korea and the first ever to count only jets among his victims. So Jabara had himself transferred to the 335th Fighter-Interceptor Squadron, which was coming in to replace his own battle-weary unit. Surely he would soon make his fifth jet kill.

Yet, unlikely as it sounds, for nearly a month he cruised through MiG Alley without even sighting a MiG; bad luck had him flying on days when the MiGs were not. In a few weeks, he would complete the 100 combat missions that would automatically send him home to the States. Then on the afternoon of May 20, as Jabara stood alert in the squadron ready room, a call came over the radio that Sabres near the Yalu had been attacked by a large force of MiGs. Jabara raced to his Sabre and blasted off the runway with the second flight of a 14-plane relief force.

On reaching the Yalu, Jabara surveyed the dogfight in front of him. About 50 MiGs had ganged up on 20 or so Sabres. Jabara punched the button to jettison his drop tanks and felt his plane lurch to the side. Just one tank had released. "Orders were that if you had a hung tank, you were to beat it for home," Jabara said later. But he was not about to lose what might be his last shot at becoming an ace. "I called my wingman and told him that we were joining the fight."

Jabara spotted three MiGs and bored straight in. Just as he was taking aim, three more swooped down from above and behind, forcing him to break off his attack. "They overshot me as I turned into them," he recalled. "Two broke away, but I latched onto the tail of the third one. He tried everything in the book to shake me, but he couldn't. I gave him three good bursts and watched the bullets hit. He did two violent snap rolls and started to spin. At about 10,000 feet the pilot bailed out. It was a good thing he did because the MiG disintegrated."

Climbing back to 20,000 feet to rejoin the battle, Jabara zeroed in on

Rivals for the skies over Korea

"Air-to-air combat at 45,000 feet is something entirely new," remarked Colonel Robert P. Baldwin, an F-86 pilot with the U.S. 51st Fighter-Interceptor Wing in Korea in 1953. "The old razzle-dazzle, ham-fisted fighter pilot is out. Now it's accurate, precision, feather-touch flying."

The Korean conflict ushered in a new era of aerial warfare, and the fighting jet emerged as the principal weapon in the struggle for air superiority. The outstanding planes of the period are displayed here and on the following pages, with the aircraft on adjacent pages in scale.

Initially, the United Nations forces relied on Lockheed F-80 Shooting Stars (below). But with the arrival of U.S. aircraft carriers, two squadrons of F9F Panthers joined the fray and later proved particularly effective as fighter-bombers. The tables were turned, however, when the Communists introduced their sweptwing MiG-15, a sleek, heavily armed jet interceptor whose outstanding combat performance came as a nasty surprise to the Americans.

To counter the MiGs, the U.S. Air Force's F-86 Sabre jet, the West's fastest fighter, was dispatched to the scene. Sabre jet pilots found that the MiG had slightly greater maneuverability and a higher service ceiling than their own planes. But the MiG also had severe shortcomings: It was far less stable than the Sabre at high speeds and had a tendency to snap out of control in right-hand turns; its gun sight was also decidedly inferior. By shrewdly taking advantage of these defects, the better-trained U.S. pilots, eventually supplied with improved Sabres, were able to rack up a kill ratio of more than 17 to 1 against the MiGs during the War's last seven months.

LOCKHEED F-80 SHOOTING STAR (1945)
America's first operational jet fighter, the F-80 was used in Korea as a ground-attack fighter-bomber after the introduction of the F-86 Sabre. Powered by a 5,400-pound-thrust Allison turbojet, it had a top speed of 560 mph and a range of 1,060 miles. Its standard armament was six nose-mounted .50-caliber machine guns and two 1,000-pound bombs. The F-80 shown here served with the 80th Fighter-Bomber Squadron.

NORTH AMERICAN F-86 SABRE (1949)
One of the classic jet fighters of all time, this
sweptwing beauty was originally designed as
a straight-wing carrier plane for the U.S.
Navy. Powered by a 5,910-pound-thrust
General Electric jet engine, it had a
top speed of 693 mph and was armed with
six .50-caliber machine guns. Almost
10,000 Sabres were built, and they served
in the air forces of 31 countries. The
Sabre seen here flew with the U.S. 51st
Fighter-Interceptor Wing in Korea.

MIKOYAN GUREVICH MIG-15 (1948)
Developed around a 5,000-pound-thrust jet of British origin, the MiG-15 marked a turning point in the evolution of Soviet military aviation and became the forerunner of a long line of high-performance jet fighters. It was armed with two 23-mm. and one 37-mm. cannon and had a top speed of 668 mph. More than 8,000 were built in Communist-bloc nations, and variants were flown by 29 countries. The one shown here belonged to the North Korean Air Force.

GRUMMAN F9F-2 PANTHER (1949)
Designed at the end of World War II, the U.S. Navy Panther was rugged, dependable and easy to maintain. With a 5,000-pound-thrust Pratt & Whitney engine, it had a maximum speed of 526 mph and a range of 1,175 miles. It carried four 20-mm. cannon and 2,000 pounds of bombs. More than 1,000 were built before the Panther was replaced by the sweptwing F9F-6 Cougar. Shown in Navy glossy sea blue camouflage, this plane bears the markings of Fighter Squadron 151 stationed aboard the U.S.S. Boxer off the Korean coast in 1953.

another MiG, one of a flight of six. "I got off two bursts and he began to smoke. He burst into flames and fell into a spin. All I could see was a whirl of fire. I had to break off then because there was another MiG on my tail." Try as he might, Jabara could not shake the MiG. "I was in big trouble," he said. Fortunately, a pair of Sabres overhead noticed his plight and shot the MiG off his tail.

By the time the battle ended, the Sabres had scored three confirmed kills and a probable fourth, and they had severely damaged five other MiGs. No Sabres had been lost. And Jabara was an ace plus one.

Several weeks later, his tour of duty over, Jabara was sent home to the U.S. But it was not long before he began to itch for the excitement of jet combat. In January 1953, Jabara volunteered to return to Korea; he rejoined the 4th Fighter Wing. Before the War was finished he would score nine additional kills, making him a jet ace three times over.

While Jabara was prowling the skies for MiGs during his first Korean assignment, U.N. troops regained the 38th Parallel and pushed beyond it, only to be thrown back. During May and June of 1951, the battle swung this way and that until, by degrees, a delicate equilibrium was established along the much-violated border. U.N. forces now had the strength to push ahead into North Korea. But with China's entry into the fight, the U.N. settled on a more limited goal: to expel the Communists from the South and restore the status quo.

To MacArthur, this stance was anathema. The role of any army is to vanquish the enemy, he believed, and he launched a one-man campaign to reverse the U.N.'s decision. "We must win," he declared in a letter read to Congress. "There is no substitute for victory." Such politicking amounted to insubordination, and President Truman promptly stripped MacArthur of his command. His replacement, Lieutenant General Matthew Ridgway, made no attempt to carry the ground war back up to the Yalu, but instead continued to pummel the Communist forces mercilessly with artillery and bombs.

By this time, the 27th Fighter-Escort Wing, equipped with F-84s, had arrived in Korea. The Thunderjets, as well as most of the other types employed as fighter-bombers, had their bomb racks modified to handle fragmentation bombs that exploded in mid-air instead of on contact with the ground. The resulting burst of shrapnel was devastating to foot soldiers, vehicles and antiaircraft batteries. On April 23, two Shooting Stars dropped four of these 260-pound devices on 200 Chinese troops caught in the open, then followed up with rockets and 3,600 rounds of .50-caliber ammunition. Nearly 90 per cent of the Chinese were wounded or killed. Altogether, on this one day alone, U.N. air strikes accounted for nearly 2,000 enemy casualties.

On July 1, 1951, as a result of such losses, the Communists agreed to discuss an armistice, and talks began nine days later in the tiny South Korean village of Kaesong; in the fall, they would move to Panmunjom.

The mere hint of an end to the fighting cooled the conflict on the ground, but in the air the War grew hotter. Bombers ranged over North Korea, pounding factories, rail yards and supply routes. The Sinuiju bridges were struck again and again but stubbornly withstood the attacks. Airfields undergoing repairs were bombed by B-29s, first at night and then, for a spell, during daylight to achieve better accuracy.

The daytime raids proved extremely costly. The Chinese now had an estimated 450 MiG-15s. On October 23, 1951, eight B-29s, escorted by F-84 Thunderjets and further protected by a screen of 34 Sabres patrolling MiG Alley, attacked a refurbished airfield at Namsi, 45 miles southeast of the Yalu. Against the American planes, the Chinese launched an interceptor force of 150 MiGs. Two thirds of this fleet kept the Sabres busy, while the remaining 50 MiGs slashed up and down at will through the B-29s and their F-84 escort. One Thunderjet and three bombers were lost; the other five B-29s all suffered major damage. The Chinese paid dearly for these kills; six MiGs were shot down during the 20-minute battle. But while the Communists could afford the fighter losses, the U.N. command had to conserve the limited number of bombers it had, and daylight raids were abandoned after this sobering experience.

Plainly more Sabres were needed to counter the MiG menace. The 4th Wing's two squadrons in Korea had fewer than 50 Sabres to throw against the Chinese fighters. Before the year's end, the 51st Fighter-Interceptor Wing stationed at Suwon would turn in its F-80 Shooting Stars for Sabres, approximately doubling the force of F-86s on guard against MiGs. But even with these reinforcements, the Sabres would still be outnumbered by 3 or 4 to 1.

The MiGs began crossing the Yalu in long trains of up to 200 aircraft, which would climb above the F-86's service ceiling of 48,000 feet and circle out of reach. For a week or more they would make no attempt to assault the American planes but would merely cruise overhead, a grand armada "waving and flashing around in the sunlight," one pilot remembered, "like a school of minnows." Then one day, several MiGs would break from the circle and attack. They would descend on the Sabres, deliver a quick burst of cannon fire and zoom back to safety, "bouncing and climbing away," said one American pilot, "like a bunch of yo-yos on a string."

Soon they began engaging in turning duels with the Americans, and at such times the sky would erupt into a vast melee of dodging and spiraling aircraft. Then, abruptly, the MiGs would return to their high-altitude patrols. It was not difficult to see that the Communists were using MiG Alley as a proving ground—giving on-the-job training to new jet pilots, exploring the performance of their planes and testing tactics.

As it turned out, these excursions were never a serious threat to the Sabres—and were hazardous in the extreme to the MiG pilots. An alert Sabre pilot could elude an attack by shoving his throttle forward and turning toward the MiG. As often as not, the MiG pilot would break off the engagement to regain altitude. If he followed the F-86 to an altitude below 25,000 feet, where the Sabre was the more maneuverable plane,

Working outdoors at a forward air base in South Korea, a team of mechanics installs a new engine in an F-86. The rear section of the airframe was attached by just four bolts; a fast-working crew could slide back the frame, change the engine and reassemble the frame in less than a hour.

the MiG pilot could find himself in serious trouble. To get on his tail, all the Sabre pilot had to do was turn sharply. Scratch one MiG.

By September 1952, some Sabre pilots had been supplied with a new model of the jet, the F-86F. With an engine that delivered nearly 15 per cent more thrust than older versions, the F model was 20 miles per hour faster than the MiG-15. The F-86F also had an improved rate of climb, though its service ceiling still remained lower than that of the MiG. The engine was not the only reason for the new jet's zip; redesigned wings helped increase the plane's speed; indeed, the new Sabre's red line was raised to Mach 1.05, though it could reach this speed only in a dive. A nine-inch extension to each wing made the plane more maneuverable above 25,000 feet. The tail had been modified as well, so that both the elevators and the entire horizontal stabilizer responded to stick movement, keeping the jet agile near the red line.

Another major improvement was a new gun sight. Before the arrival of the F-86F, the Sabre pilot, having set his sight for the range to his target, had to fly a fairly constant distance from it. But doing so was difficult once the battle had begun. A new sight, called the A-1, monitored range by means of a radar housed in the plane's nose. The pilot had only to hold the sight on his target for the one second required to lock onto it. Then regardless of whether he closed the range or opened it, the sight enabled him to aim the guns accurately.

The new Sabres had an immediate effect on the air war. In each of the 10 months after their introduction, at least 25 MiGs were shot down. Sabre losses declined about 10 per cent during the same period. Even so, a MiG would occasionally give one of the new Sabres a tremendous duel. In such cases, the pilots suspected that the MiGs were being flown by Russians. The suspicion was confirmed on July 4, 1952, when a Sabre pilot pulled alongside a stricken MiG, glanced into the cockpit and saw an opponent with a ruddy face and bushy red eyebrows. And it may well have been a Russian that Major Robinson Risner tangled with on December 4, when four MiGs rose up to meet his flight of four Sabres.

"Seeing one another about the same time," recalled Risner, "both the MiG flight and my flight dropped tanks," and the battle was on. In the first turn, Risner fired a short burst that struck one MiG's canopy, and then he closed in for the kill. The enemy pilot rolled out of the way, hung upside down a moment, then dived. Risner roared down in pursuit. "This is going to be the easiest kill I ever had!" he remembered radioing to his wingman. "I just knew he was going to splatter."

But at the last instant, the MiG leveled off and shot along a dry riverbed. "He was so low he was throwing up small rocks," Risner recalled. As the MiG began to climb again, Risner said, "I dropped down to get him, but to hit him I had to get down in his jet wash. He'd chop the throttle and throw out his speed brakes. I would coast up beside him, wingtip to wingtip." Glancing into the cockpit, Risner could see that his opponent had a light complexion but could not be certain he was Russian. "When it looked like I was going to overshoot him," Risner continued, "I'd roll over the top and come down on the other side of him. When I did, he'd go into a hard turn, pulling all the Gs he could. This guy was one fantastic pilot."

At one point the MiG rolled onto its back and flipped over the top of a small mountain, but the Sabre stayed with him. "I was having a real difficult time," acknowledged Risner, but every now and again a gun burst would connect. The MiG's canopy flew off, then a shred of tail; flames licked back along the left side. As Risner coasted alongside again, the pilot, wearing a leather helmet, looked over and shook his fist.

By now the battle had crossed the Yalu and Risner found himself flying deep into Manchuria, forbidden territory. The MiG was leading Risner—and his wingman, First Lieutenant Joe Logan, who had hung on throughout—straight for a Chinese airfield and its antiaircraft batteries. The MiG skimmed low toward the airstrip and cut sharply between two hangars. Risner followed, guns blazing. The MiG made two circuits of the field, then sank to the grass along the runway. Moving at more than 400 miles per hour and riddled with bullet holes, the jet sim-

A formation of F-84 Thunderjets—each plane carrying two 500-pound bombs in wing racks—heads toward a target in North Korea. Thunderjets flew more than 86,000 bombing sorties during the War and later became the first fighter-bombers to carry tactical nuclear weapons.

ply broke apart. "Little pieces flew everywhere," Risner recalled.

His kill accomplished, Risner and his wingman had to withdraw through the flak, and Logan took a hit in a fuel tank. Now came the most extraordinary feat of the entire mission. When Logan's tanks had drained virtually dry, Risner told him to shut off his engine. Then, Risner, taking care not to block his Sabre's air intake, eased the nose of his plane into the tailpipe of the other Sabre and pushed his crippled companion 100 miles to Cho-do Island, off the coast of North Korea in the Yellow Sea. There Logan would be nearly certain of rescue by American ships and planes on station. He bailed out, and Risner flew back to Suwon to report his kill. Despite Risner's heroic effort, Logan did not make it. After punching out over the Yellow Sea, he drowned before he could be picked up.

Firmly in control of the air over North Korea, U.N. bomber and fighter-bomber pilots disrupted every Communist attempt to mass for a major offensive. The aviators blasted key bridges and road intersections, causing traffic jams of supply trucks that made easy pickings. They destroyed

Snaring a MiG with a bundle of cash

On April 26, 1953, two B-29s dropped an unusual payload on Communist positions along the Yalu River: one million leaflets announcing a $50,000 reward and political asylum to any pilot who delivered a MiG-15 into American hands.

Five months passed with no response. Then airmen at Kimpo Airfield outside Seoul were startled to see a North Korean MiG-15 come in for a landing. Lieutenant Ro Kum Suk had just defected with a MiG-15BIS, the model most frequently encountered in the skies over Korea. Despite his claim that he knew nothing of the bounty, Ro got the full $50,000, plus a $50,000 bonus, and the Americans got a priceless opportunity to study every inch of the Soviet jet.

The MiG's 37-mm. and 23-mm. cannon are lowered for inspection.

Bearing U.S. markings, the captured MiG awaits testing. Said a pilot who flew it: "I could whip it with an F-86 any day in the week."

963 locomotives during the War, rendering North Korea's rail system all but useless. The Communists were forced to abandon their basic strategy—to use the peace negotiations as a screen for reviving the conflict.

In late May 1953, two years after the talks had begun, the Communists decided to come to terms with the U.N. But in an attempt to force the most favorable settlement possible, the Chinese lashed out on the ground and in the air. Shielded from air strikes by bad weather in May, they prepared huge last-ditch assaults. The first came in June, the second in July. Fortunately in each instance, clouds thinned as the attacks got under way, allowing the jets—along with virtually every other combat plane in Korea—to parry the thrusts. The result was the loss by the Communists of thousands upon thousands of troops. During the same months, the MiGs launched a final air offensive. They flew more sorties, fought more aggressively and suffered more losses than at virtually any other hour of the War. In May, 56 MiGs were shot down; in June, 77.

One man who flew against them would end up as the top-scoring ace of the Korean War—one kill ahead of Jabara. He was Captain Joseph McConnell Jr., a 31-year-old veteran of World War II. Turned down for pilot training because the Army Air Forces needed bombardiers and navigators, he spent World War II guiding B-17s on raids over Germany. When that conflict ended he applied again to become a pilot and was accepted. He was flying Shooting Stars in Alaska at the outbreak of the Korean War, and for two frustrating years he pestered his superiors with requests for a transfer to the combat zone.

Finally, in late 1952, McConnell was trained to fly the F-86 and shipped out to Suwon, joining the 51st Fighter-Interceptor Wing. He began racking up kills almost immediately. On February 16, 1953, he shot down his fifth MiG. By mid-April he had dispatched four more and had locked his gun sight on the 10th when a MiG clobbered him from behind. He was plucked unharmed from the Yellow Sea, and the next day was at the controls of another Sabre. On April 24 he became a double ace; then during four days in May, from the 13th to the 16th, he shot down three more MiGs.

On May 18, McConnell matched that score. He was on Yalu patrol. Four MiG-15s, apparently unaware that the Sabres were there, crossed directly in front of them. Within seconds McConnell was on the tail of an enemy wingman, ripping into his fuselage with machine-gun fire. He followed the MiG as it dived for safety, peppering it with short bursts. "I saw the canopy come off and the pilot bail out," he reported. "I watched the MiG crash far below."

While McConnell was thus occupied, the wingman's leader maneuvered onto the American's tail. "Man, he was close!" McConnell remembered. "I could hear the cannon just thumping away at me. The tracers look like great big balls of fire heading your way." Wildly dodging the projectiles, McConnell broke into a sharp turn and succeeded in cutting behind his adversary. With several hundred rounds of .50-caliber fire pumped into it, the MiG began to smoke, but its pilot was not

giving up yet. As McConnell closed in, the Communist pilot, climbing from below, pulled up in an effort to ram. Only a last-second swerve to one side allowed McConnell to escape. McConnell watched as the MiG flipped over and spun in. Low on fuel, he headed for base.

That very afternoon, McConnell led another flight north. This time the Sabres were bounced from above by four enemy fighters. Two of them purposely overshot the American planes, attempting to lure them into an attack, while the other two MiGs came in from the rear. It was a cunning gambit, but it did not work. McConnell, having anticipated the ruse, knew just how to counter it. He allowed the first pair of planes to sweep on by and went after the second pair. "I jumped on the tail of one of them," he said, "and really poured the fire into him. The pilot then pulled up, opened his speed brakes and bailed out." It was McConnell's third kill of the day—his last of the War—and it raised his total score to 16.

On July 27, 1953, Captain Ralph Parr, a Sabre ace with nine kills, was escorting a final reconnaissance mission over North Korea. After two years of diplomatic maneuver, punctuated by fruitless infantry assaults whenever talks broke off, a cease-fire had been arranged for 10 p.m. After that hour, neither side would be allowed to increase its forces in Korea. Consequently, the Communists had been moving MiGs south from China in order to have as many as possible inside Korea when the shooting stopped. The reconnaissance mission was to count the jets so that any augmentation of them after the cease-fire could be noted.

No MiGs had challenged the mission, but shortly after the planes turned toward Kimpo, Parr spotted an Il-2 piston-engined transport about 20,000 feet below him. Double-checking to make sure that he had not crossed the Yalu, Parr dived, pulled in behind his unsuspecting victim and fired two bursts. The Il-2 began to burn, banked away, then crashed. It was the last Sabre kill of the War.

Hours later the shooting stopped, and the Korean War was over. By driving the North Koreans and Chinese out of the South, the U.N. had accomplished all that it had set out to do three years earlier. Much of this success had sprung directly from U.N. air superiority over the battlefield, without which, as the Chinese themselves asserted in several captured documents, U.N. troops would have been pushed into the sea. And air superiority, for the first time, had become the responsibility of fighting jets. They had seized control of Korean airspace wherever they appeared. They had performed with distinction as interceptors, as escorts, as reconnaissance planes and as fighter-bombers in support of ground troops. In MiG Alley, the Sabres had met a more numerous adversary and outfought him at every turn. In all, they brought down 792 MiG-15s, for a loss of only 78 F-86s. With aircraft so closely matched it was dramatic proof that in the jet age, as before, it was the men at the controls, as much as the quality of the planes they flew, that would determine the margin of victory or defeat. ⌁

Photographs of the 39 American aces of the Korean War are arrayed as playing cards in this composite portrait. For each pilot, the total number of victories is given below his picture. The two highest-scoring aces, Captain Joseph McConnell Jr. and Major James Jabara, flank the map.

A gun's-eye view of battle

"Like olden knights," said jet ace Colonel Harry Thyng, "the F-86 pilots ride up over North Korea, the sun glistening off silver aircraft, contrails streaming behind as they challenge the enemy to come up and fight." To Colonel Thyng and many of the other American pilots of the Korean War, encounters with Soviet-made MiG-15s were the modern equivalent of the medieval joust—with the combatants charging at each other at a combined speed of more than 1,200 mph.

Most of the battles between F-86s and MiG-15s took place several miles above the swath of land near the Yalu River known as MiG Alley. There, American and Communist pilots fought quicksilver encounters that could virtually begin and end in the blink of an eye. The deadly results of these jet-age dogfights were recorded by gun cameras equipped with shutters that were triggered automatically when the pilot fired his weapons.

The gun cameras' grainy photographs—seen at right and on the following pages—were enlarged from motion-picture film to produce a pilot's-eye view of jet combat for intelligence officers to study and interpret. The pictures also offered proof positive of a pilot's claim to victory— evidence without which many a kill would have had to go into the records as merely a probable.

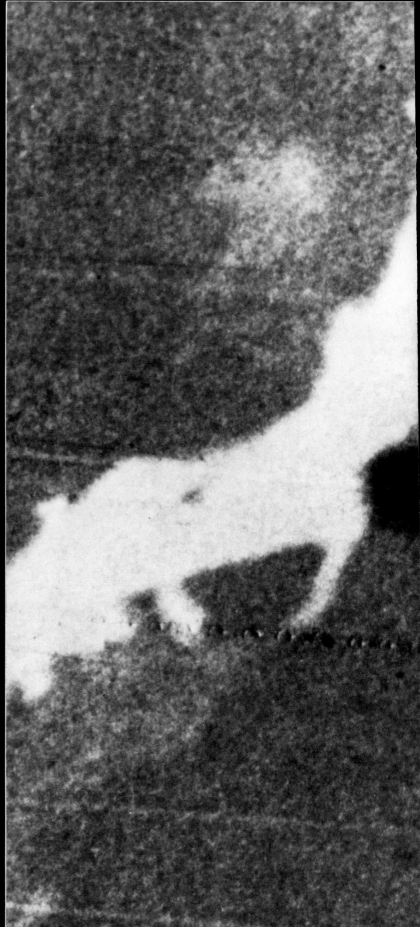

A gun camera mounted in an F-86 captures the final moments of a MiG-15 as the Communist jet, trailing smoke and flames, plunges toward the Yalu River after a February 1953 dogfight.

Photographed by a pursuing F-86, a damaged MiG-15 attacks a second Sabre jet in this remarkable sequence, which reads from top to bottom on each page. Trailing smoke, the doomed MiG fires a rocket that hits the Sabre's left wing (this page, bottom). Part of the wing flies off (opposite page, top), and the American jet begins to spin out of control in the final two frames.

A MiG-15 pilot ejects from his aircraft seconds after it was hit by gunfire from an F-86 during a May 1953 dogfight. The pilot of the Sabre, whose gun camera recorded this sequence, was Lieutenant Edwin E. Aldrin Jr., who would walk on the moon 16 years later as an Apollo 11 astronaut.

Triple jet ace Captain James Jabara pursues a fleeing MiG-15 (opposite, top). After hitting the plane, Jabara took a gun-camera photograph of the enemy pilot parachuting to earth (opposite, bottom) in order to confirm his kill.

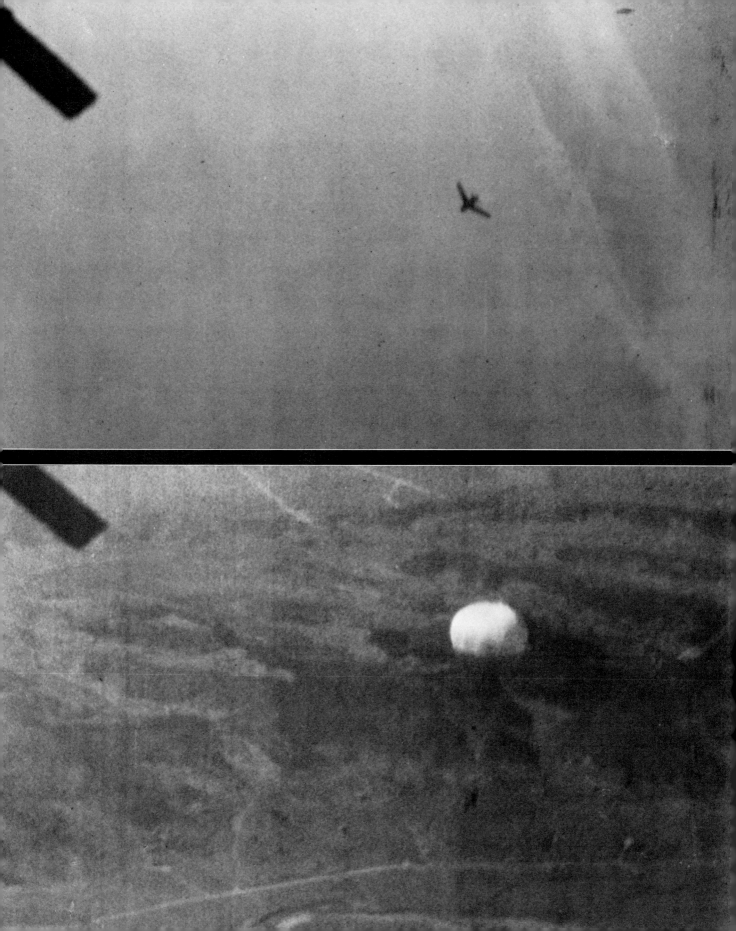

3

The Strategic Air Command: bombers for peace

The B-47 Stratojet took off from the United States Air Force Base at Sidi Slimane in French Morocco and headed for England. When it arrived there, foul weather made a landing impossible, so the pilot turned the sweptwing bomber around and flew home. But as the plane was approaching the base, one member of the crew said, "Let's go back to England, where we're supposed to go." They radioed for a tanker to come up and refuel them. Over England, they found the weather no better, but now as an exercise they decided not to land but instead to see how long they could stay in the air. With official blessing, they flew back and forth between the two countries, refueling when necessary, until they had been aloft 47 hours and 35 minutes and had traveled a distance of 21,163 miles.

The year was 1954, the Korean War was over and the stunt served an important purpose. It showed just how long the arm of the United States was. It also demonstrated the mettle of the crew, who during their endless flight, strapped into their steel seats and unable to move about, had had little or no sleep. The B-47, then the world's fastest bomber, belonged to the Strategic Air Command, or SAC, the United States' global peace-keeping force. SAC's bombers regularly roamed the skies, taking off from bases around the globe, their bellies loaded with atomic bombs—a fearsomely efficient nuclear force "at war against war," as its members liked to say.

In charge of this elite group was Lieutenant General Curtis E. LeMay, a brusque, cigar-chomping veteran of World War II. He had led some of the first daylight bombing raids over Hitler's Germany and then, as head of XXI Bomber Command on Guam, he initiated a series of daring low-altitude incendiary attacks on Japanese cities. The devastation these attacks produced was unequaled in the history of warfare, yet LeMay had never flinched from making up his mind to go ahead with them. "*My* decision and *my* order," he said. "There must be a commander."

When LeMay took over late in 1948, SAC was in a sorry state. It had been founded on March 21, 1946, to conduct "long range offensive operations in any part of the world" as well as "maximum range reconnaissance." But because of a lack of funds and a general mood of

Armed with two nuclear-tipped Hound Dog air-to-surface missiles, a B-52 heavy bomber of the U.S. Air Force's Strategic Air Command undergoes refueling beneath a KC-135 tanker.

peacetime lassitude, the fledgling Strategic Air Command was allowed to operate at such an inefficient level that it scarcely qualified as a military outfit. "The Air Force had gone to utter hell," LeMay wrote angrily. "We didn't have one crew, *not one* crew in the entire command who could do a professional job. Not one of the outfits was up to strength—neither in airplanes nor in people, nor in anything else."

At one California base, the operations room was used primarily for playing cards. As often as not, training missions were a shambles. On one mission, a mock attack on New York City in 1947, nearly one fourth of the 131 bombers involved failed to leave the runway because of supply problems and sloppy maintenance. The rest reached New York in various states of disorder, ran the simulated bombing runs with manifest imprecision and returned to a gloomy appraisal at base. When LeMay took charge, he ordered a similar attack on Dayton, Ohio, and the results were equally embarrassing. None of the airplanes finished the mission as briefed. With bulldog determination, he began putting machines and men to rights.

One of LeMay's first moves was to strengthen and modernize SAC's aged bomber fleet. Neither the World War II-vintage Boeing B-29s nor the slightly updated model known as the B-50 had, in his view, enough range. And they were too slow; neither could fly 400 miles per hour. More to LeMay's liking was the gigantic B-36, which entered service in 1950. With six piston pusher engines, a 162-foot fuselage and a 230-foot wingspan, the B-36 was one of the largest bombers ever built. It had taken nearly six years to develop and was so expensive that it threatened to drain the nation's limited military budget. But to LeMay the B-36, with its combat radius of more than 3,500 miles, was the very aircraft his country needed. To supplement those that SAC already had, he persuaded the Air Force to order 86 more. And to boost their speed from 381 miles per hour to 435 miles per hour, engineers equipped each with four auxiliary turbojets in pods under the wings. Then, looking ahead, LeMay fixed his attention on a pair of all-jet bombers still under development.

Furthest along in 1949 was the six-engined Boeing B-47 Stratojet, a prototype of which had first flown in 1947. It was a beautiful airplane, with its sleek fuselage and sweptback wings. And SAC crews found it a joy to fly, "almost fighter-like in its flying qualities," as one pilot put it. The B-47 had one drawback. With a full load—18,000 gallons of fuel and 10,000 pounds of bombs—it could not reach Moscow without refueling. But since it was the only all-jet bomber available, the Air Force ordered it in huge quantities. More than 1,800 would be delivered to SAC by 1957. And, if the B-47's unrefueled range was limited, it was better than nothing. Besides, as the crew that had kept their B-47 in the air for almost two days had demonstrated, in-flight refueling could effectively extend its range, enabling LeMay to send the bomber to any distant target he chose.

The other jet was Boeing's mammoth B-52 Stratofortress. Intended

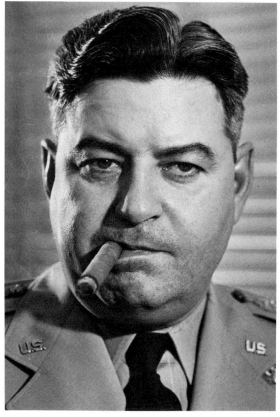

Cigar clamped between his teeth, General Curtis E. LeMay projects single-minded resolve. As chief of the Strategic Air Command from 1948 to 1957, he made combat readiness a religion at SAC. "My determination," he wrote, "was to put everyone in SAC into this frame of mind: We are at war now."

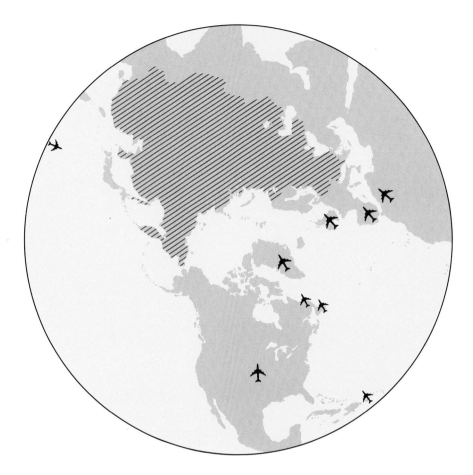

This map shows SAC's global deployment at its peak in 1957, when it operated 38 bases in the United States and another 30 overseas, located in countries marked on the map at right by bomber symbols. Smaller planes indicate countries with a single base; larger planes indicate those with more than one base, such as Great Britain, which had 15 SAC installations.

as a heavy intercontinental bomber to replace the B-36, it took a frustratingly long time to develop. The designers had started the planning in 1946, beginning with a fairly conventional straight-wing aircraft driven by four turboprop engines. From there they tried more than 30 different combinations of engine, wing shape and gross weight, searching for an aircraft that would be light for its size, have low drag and plenty of lifting power.

Then one memorable Friday in 1948, after a marathon conference with Air Force procurement officers at Dayton, Ohio, Boeing's top design team abandoned earlier plans and retired to a hotel room for a think session. They emerged on Monday with a 33-page proposal for an entirely new bomber. It had immense, drooping, sweptback wings from which hung eight Pratt & Whitney J57 turbojets in double pods. Its hulking appearance on the ground would earn it the acronym BUFF, which, in bowdlerized translation, stood for ''Big Ugly Fat Fellow.'' But once airborne, the B-52 turned into an object of soaring beauty. And when it finally became available in 1955, it was everything LeMay could wish. Fast (more than 600-mile-per-hour cruising speed), potent (up to 75,000 pounds of bombload), long-ranged (more than 6,000 miles), it would carry anything from 500-pound conventional bombs to thermonuclear weapons. Moreover, this firepower could be delivered from eight miles up, or higher, beyond effective range of antiaircraft guns.

In a rocket-assisted takeoff, a B-47 bomber leaps aloft during a 1954 exercise. The rockets, mounted externally on the aft fuselage, delivered an additional 33,000 pounds of thrust for takeoff when the 206,700-pound jet was carrying a heavy payload. Once airborne, the pilot jettisoned the rocket canisters.

But the B-52 would not undergo its first test flights until 1952, and in the meantime LeMay concentrated his energies upon SAC's flight crews and ground personnel. He had resolved at the outset to whip them into the toughest, most professional fighting force in U.S. military history.

It was an awesome task and the general went about it in an awesome manner. He imposed draconian discipline and a brutal schedule of training on the airmen. Each SAC unit was treated to a grueling round of proficiency exercises designed to bring it up to razor-sharp combat readiness—and keep it there. Work weeks of 70 or 80 hours became routine. Every morning the ground crews would run through an exhaustive countdown on the aircraft assigned to them, checking out all systems to make sure the planes were ready to go at any moment. Flight crews were engaged in round-the-clock exercises—some lasting 24 hours—that simulated attacks on Soviet targets. Radar signals from the aircraft took the place of live bombs, and the accuracy of the hits was registered by receiving stations on the ground. By 1957 every American city of 25,000 or more inhabitants had been subjected to these radar assaults. San Francisco was bombed more than 600 times in one month.

Practice missions were planned with all the attention to detail of a wartime raid. Courses, altitudes, speeds and fuel consumption were calculated to the second for each leg in the flight plan. Aircraft commanders and their crews underwent as much as three hours of briefing

before each flight; pilots and navigators memorized approach routes, arrival times and radar profiles of their targets. Takeoffs were executed with dazzling precision. One amazed civilian watched a wing of 26 B-47s depart from the Sidi Slimane air base in French Morocco; he reported that each plane lifted off exactly 55 seconds after its predecessor, at almost exactly the same speed and from a nearly identical spot on the runway. Actual flight times of many missions stretched out to 15 hours, during which the planes were refueled in the air.

LeMay's training program made it clear that the responsibility for team precision lay with the teams themselves. He did not tolerate failure for any reason; he was, he said, "unable to distinguish between the unfortunate and the incompetent." Upon returning from each mission, the fliers had to sit through debriefings and assessments that could last for hours. The general instituted a rating system in which crews were evaluated for efficiency and skill. A high score brought select crews temporary spot promotions with higher pay; should performance drop even once, the promotions would be rescinded.

On the theory that every SAC unit should be prepared to take off at a moment's notice, LeMay had elaborate bombproof underground alert facilities and living quarters built. Here the men stayed for days at a time. They slept in their flight suits and carried pocket beepers that would send them racing for their airplanes. Within 15 minutes of the alarm, they had to be airborne. "Somebody might blow the whistle on us tomorrow morning," the general declared. "I will order my crews out in those airplanes, and I expect to be in the first one myself."

The men knew that they had a great deal more chance of surviving in the event of nuclear war than did their families, and this knowledge was a difficult burden for them. The strain, coupled with that of their missions, colored their lives. A typical B-47 crew might be aloft 15 hours, flying a distance of 8,000 miles. The plane was so crowded with electronic gadgets and extra fuel that there was room for only three men. Their heads were encased in steel-and-glass helmets, making it impossible for them to scratch their ears or blow their noses. Their bodies were sheathed in clinging rubber-and-nylon skins designed to inflate in a sudden decompression of the cabin. They sat the whole while on their survival packs, which were stuffed with such items as food, fishhooks, a folding shotgun and an ax. Over the course of a mission, they dehydrated, losing five pounds or more weight in the thin, dry air of the stratosphere. And when they landed, exhausted, their nerves frayed, they found the time they had to spend with their wives and children all too short; they had always to be ready for another mission, often on a moment's notice. In addition to such stresses, SAC crews were obliged to endure the hardships imposed by poor pay and inadequate housing, and not surprisingly the net result of all this was the breakup of many of their marriages.

LeMay's sense of urgency was fueled, of course, by the developing nuclear standoff between the Soviet Union and the U.S. In 1953, the Russians had exploded a hydrogen bomb in central Siberia. Nearly 10 months had passed since the U.S. had set off its first large thermonuclear device. LeMay tirelessly lobbied Congress for funds to buy more bombers and to create new air bases, both in the U.S. and overseas, and he called for a massive increase in nuclear payload. His apocalyptic sense of mission, far from alienating his men, infused them with a sense of dedication. Young copilots began chomping cigars in imitation of their boss. They recognized, as their pride grew, that they were part of what the general called "a wonderful, complex and beautiful instrument."

By 1955, SAC counted more than 3,000 aircraft, lodged in a worldwide network of 51 bases, from Maine to North Africa, and from Guam to Great Britain. Of these 3,000 planes, 1,309 were nuclear bombers. Another 568 were long-range fighters, Republic's swept-wing F-84F Thunderjet. There were also 761 tankers and 51 transports. The most vital of SAC's support planes was the prop-driven Boeing KC-97 tanker, a kind of aerial filling station that permitted bombers to refuel in mid-flight. The KC-97 extended the bombers' scope dramatically. Every six minutes, LeMay liked to boast, a SAC aircraft was being refueled in the air. And this meant that in periods of international crisis, every minute of the day and night, there was a SAC bomber somewhere in the sky.

In May 1956, six months after the Soviets tested their first airborne H-bomb, the U.S. was ready to make an experimental drop of one of its own. The bomber had to be capable of a huge payload—early thermonuclear bombs weighed as much as 42,000 pounds and took up 1,525 square feet of space. And the bomber had to be able to escape the blast. The shock wave would be of such speed and power that it might well disable the plane. The B-52 was the natural choice.

Preparations for the test progressed with much public fanfare, along with utmost secrecy as to specific details. A B-52 from the 4930th Test Group stationed at Eniwetok in the west central Pacific was picked out, and a crew from Kirtland Air Force Base near Albuquerque, New Mexico, was selected and given special training. They had to be able to follow the flight plan precisely; everything depended on exact timing. Practice bombing was done with both visual and radar backup, and ground monitoring as well.

The test date was set for early May but had to be postponed because of bad weather. Finally, well before dawn on May 21, Major David M. Critchlow of Sacramento, California, commander of the mission, climbed into the cockpit of the B-52 poised on Eniwetok's runway. He ran through an elaborate countdown with the pilot, Major Charles Smith, and then, with all systems go and the bomb cradled in its bay 20 feet behind their seats, they thundered down the runway and into the air, heading up through the darkness. With navigator-bombardier Major Dwight E. Durner plotting the approach, the jet quickly reached its target, tiny Namu island in the Bikini atoll, 200 miles east of Eniwetok.

A crossed pattern of lights on the ground marked the bull's-eye. Smith passed once over the target at 50,000 feet, then doubled back along a predetermined figure-8 course. All the while, Durner fed in computer corrections for altitude, velocity and wind direction. As the jet approached the release point, Durner lined up the cross hairs of his automatic bombsight on the bull's-eye. At 5:50 a.m. precisely a red light blinked on, the bomb-bay doors opened and the bomb dropped clear.

The immense bomb hurtled downward in a long, arcing trajectory, propelled by the momentum of the plane's 600-mile-per-hour speed, heading for its detonation point seven miles ahead and 15,000 feet above the ocean. At the same moment, Smith performed a breakaway maneuver, whipping the bomber into a 180-degree turn and losing altitude to maintain air speed. The bomb fell for 60 seconds. Then it exploded. An unearthly light filled the cockpit, and the jet began to bounce about in the turbulence. But by now it was 15 miles from the detonation site and well out of danger. To all intents and purposes, the whole operation had been a resounding success.

But in the weeks that followed, news leaked out that the test had not been perfect after all. The bomb had not come close to Namu, it seemed, but had fallen wide of its mark by nearly four miles. Under the stress of the moment, the bombardier, in correcting for wind drift, had apparently done so twice—first during the dry run over the target, and again just before the release. As a result, the bomb missed the target.

The fact that there had been an error inspired anxious questions the world over. What would happen if an H-bomb misfired? What would be the consequences if an H-bomb or an A-bomb were dropped by mistake, through some mechanical defect or human misjudgment? What if the bomber carrying the bomb should crash?

Under LeMay's exacting command the accident rate at SAC had been cut to an exemplary minimum—from 65 to three or four aircraft lost or badly damaged for every 100,000 hours of flying time. Most lapses occurred during training exercises in which no nuclear weapons were carried. But even with the most stringent safeguards, mishaps sometimes did take place. No one outside the military heard about them until one fine afternoon in March 1958, when an explosion rocked the small community of Mars Bluff, South Carolina. The blast was less than apocalyptic, but it tore a large hole in the backyard vegetable garden of railroad conductor Walter Gregg and blew the roof off his house.

A SAC B-47 carrying an atomic bomb had been flying over South Carolina on a regular mission when the shackle holding the bomb in place failed. The bomb had not been armed and therefore could not go off, but the TNT charge it contained, used to activate its nuclear components, most definitely could. A crewman tried frantically to secure the bomb. But as he was working, the shackle gave way

SAC B-52 air crews are saluted at Castle Air Force Base, California, after completing a 1957 round-the-world flight in a record-setting 45 hours 19

minutes. The bombers were refueled five times in the air.

entirely and the bomb dropped out. It hit Gregg's vegetable patch, and the TNT exploded.

An embarrassed government was quick to point out the fail-safe nature of the bomb. "The explosion of this weapon demonstrates the accuracy of the recent Department of Defense statement that there would be no nuclear explosion involved in the detonation of an unarmed bomb," announced Secretary of Defense Neil H. McElroy. Then he added, "I can only say that these are perilous times."

The bombing of Mars Bluff sent a shock wave of protest through Europe and Asia. People asked: Could a freak nuclear blast by one side or the other accidentally trigger World War III?

SAC answered with a firm "Negative." It pointed to a rigorous set of command procedures. Assuming that if any system can go wrong it probably will, SAC had built so many checks and balances into the handling and delivery of airborne nuclear weapons that chances of an unintended firing were reduced to nil. Nothing could accidentally start a war, SAC claimed—not mechanical failure, not garbled communications, not a crazed jet pilot out to smash Russia on his own. Members of the lead, or select, crews—those assigned to deliver nuclear weapons to specific targets—were carefully screened, given psychological tests and trained to the keenest edge of proficiency. Before each flight the plane's commander received a locked orange box containing maps, codes, radar information and the sequence that activated the bomb's arming mechanism. After a preflight inventory, the box would remain locked unless the commander was told, by coded radio message from SAC headquarters at Offutt Air Force Base near Omaha, Nebraska, or SAC's airborne command center, to open it. Should the order come, he would need the assistance of two other crew members to break the seals, turn the knobs and close the circuits that would activate the weapon.

Similar precautions were taken regarding the bomber's flight plan. Not only was every mile of the route worked out in advance, but the flight would be monitored throughout by ground radar stations. Any deviation from the scheduled flight plan would be questioned immediately. If it seemed that a pilot was traveling without orders toward the Soviet Union, a pair of jet fighters from the nearest U.S. Air Force base would be dispatched to intercept him.

As a further precaution, SAC set up an invisible barrier known as the Fail-Safe line and designated it as the outermost limit of its bomber operations. No armed SAC bomber could cross it without a specific order from the President. The order would be sent, in code, to SAC's commander and checked by a return call to the President. It would then be relayed to the alert bombers that, in a crisis, would already be in the air, awaiting instructions. Two commands would be needed, both double-checked by radio call-backs. The first would send the bombers streaking toward the Fail-Safe line, and the second, the Go code, would tell them to cross it. If the bombers reached the demarcation line without receiving the Go code, they would automatically turn back.

No SAC bombers had ever been ordered to carry nuclear payloads across the line, but a number of specialized SAC jets darted over it with some frequency. They were reconnaissance planes, modified to carry cameras or electronic intelligence equipment in place of bombs. The mission was to fly surveillance flights around the edge of the Soviet Union in order to ferret out information on its radar defense system, including numbers and frequencies. And as these planes approached the Soviet Union's borders, they often came into direct confrontation with Russian jets, just as their Russian counterparts did whenever they flew close to the U.S.

In one flight of this type, on July 1, 1960, Major Willard G. Palm guided an RB-47 reconnaissance bomber over the icy Barents Sea off the Soviet Union's northern Arctic coast. In the seat behind him, copilot Captain F. Bruce Olmstead scanned the sky for Russian aircraft. Down in the bomb bay, in a sealed compartment crammed with radarscopes, computers, electronic listening devices and navigation equipment, three electronic-warfare officers were monitoring the Russian radar net.

Palm swept eastward parallel to the Kola Peninsula, keeping well offshore to avoid straying inadvertently into Soviet airspace. His navigator, Captain John R. McKone, crouching over a tiny desk in the bomber's nose, called over the intercom to verify their position: 50 miles north of the coast and approaching Holy Nose Cape, a prominent landmark on the peninsula. In a few minutes Palm would start a slow turn to the left that would carry him north, away from the Cape.

Just then Palm heard the voice of copilot Olmstead calling over the intercom: "Bill, check right wing. We got a stranger at 3 o'clock high." It was not unusual for ferret planes to draw out interceptors on such missions. So Palm was not particularly concerned to find himself being trailed by a Soviet MiG.

"Keep your eye on him," he ordered. He called for another position check to make sure the bomber was still over international waters, and a few moments later the MiG disappeared.

But not for long. Palm was already starting his turn when the same MiG or another streaked in from the right. It came so close that it almost brushed the RB-47's wing tip as Palm banked for the turn. "Where in hell did that guy come from?" he asked. The MiG broke away, circled back and bore in fast from the rear, opening fire. The shells ripped across the bomber's left wing.

The RB-47 was armed with two remote-controlled tail-turret 20-millimeter cannon operated by Olmstead. He attempted to return the Russian's fire, using his radar to aim, but the MiG was now so close that it filled his entire radarscope, producing a confused image. He switched to visual firing and tried to draw a bead, but he was too late. The bomber, with two of its three port engines now spitting fire from the Russian's hits, lurched into a flat spin. It took all Olmstead's skill and concentration to help Palm wrestle with the flight controls. "Stand by! Stand by!" the major shouted to his crew. Meanwhile, the MiG circled back to pour in another burst of cannon fire. Long streamers of flame erupted from the bomber's wing and licked back along the left side of the fuselage. Palm did not hesitate. "Bail out! Bail out!" he ordered.

Parachuting from a jet bomber at 30,000 feet is not a simple matter. The crew member presses a trigger on a handle next to his seat to eject, and an explosive charge propels him into space with numbing force. He hits the plane's slip stream—a seven-mile-a-minute hurricane for a jet traveling at 480 miles per hour—and then must free-fall almost three miles to 14,000 feet before his speed is slowed by the atmosphere to the point where the chute can open safely.

With the fire raging and the bomber quickly becoming unflyable, Olmstead had no option but to eject. The force of his exit caused him to black out and crushed one of his vertebrae. At 14,000 feet his parachute opened automatically with a violent jolt, slowing his fall speed from 140 miles per hour to 15. He came to several hundred yards above the water, just in time to release his survival kit and self-inflating life raft. When he hit the surface, he unstrapped his chute and, despite the pain from his broken back, hauled himself through the freezing sea to the raft. As he climbed aboard, another parachute dropped into the rough water nearby. McKone had also bailed out. He too had been unconscious for several moments but he had escaped injury and was able to scramble into his life raft.

American radar trackers followed the burning jet for another 20 minutes. Palm apparently bailed out too but did not live. The Russians found his body three days later and returned it to the Americans; he was buried with full military honors at Arlington National Cemetery. The fate of the electronic-warfare officers is not known.

Olmstead and McKone were picked up by a Russian trawler after six and a half hours in the water and were held for seven months. They were accused of spying and of violating Soviet airspace—although the observations of American radar stations following the flight showed that they clearly had not done so. In fact, it was evident to all that the Soviet pilot, a Captain Vasily A. Polyakov, had violated a basic standing order in his own command by attacking a plane over international waters. Polyakov's motives were never made clear. Perhaps he had been seized by a sudden rash belligerence; perhaps he had been confused as to his position. In any case, Olmstead and McKone were delivered home on January 24, 1961, in a Russian good-will gesture just four days after the inauguration of President John F. Kennedy.

Flying the Soviet perimeter was the most obviously perilous activity SAC planes undertook, but routine missions carried their own dangers, inherent in the handling of giant jet planes. Among the most tension-filled moments in any mission were the 20 minutes or so when a jet bomber pulled up about 20 feet aft and below an aerial tanker's tail to take on fuel. Extreme precision was required, both from the bomber's pilot and navigator, and from the crew operating the tanker.

In-flight refueling was particularly hazardous in SAC's early days, when the tankers were the prop-driven KC-97s, lumbering craft whose top speed, when they were fully loaded, was dangerously close to the stalling speed of the B-47s and B-52s. To give the tankers maximum speed, refueling operations were often performed in a shallow dive. After 1957, SAC began to replace the KC-97s with new KC-135 jet tankers, which had been developed by Boeing from the same proto- type that led to the company's 707 airliner and which were capable of speeds up to 600 miles an hour. When both bombers and tankers were able to cruise comfortably together, the procedure became some- what simpler. But for two giant aircraft bobbing about in a rolling ocean of air, in-flight refueling was never easy. Inevitably, there were acci- dents. Most have caused little stir, but one sent another flash of nuclear fear around the world.

On the 16th of January, 1966, a B-52 loaded with four unarmed 1.5-megaton hydrogen bombs lifted off from Seymour Johnson Air Force Base in North Carolina and headed out on a routine mis- sion. The plane carried its lethal cargo toward the southwestern corner of the Soviet Union, patrolled near the border for nine or 10 hours and started home. Then disaster. During refueling the next morning over southeastern Spain, the B-52 somehow collid- ed with its KC-135 tanker. Villagers in Palomares, 30,000 feet be- low, saw a flash and a huge fireball. Chunks of flaming debris, some of them larger than the villagers' houses, came raining down on Palomares and the nearby tomato and bean fields. Seven of the Americans died—three crewmen from the bomber, and all four men from the tanker. Four others from the B-52 ejected safely and drifted

in their parachutes out to sea, where they were picked up by fishermen.

But then there was the matter of the B-52s' four missing H-bombs. Three were found within a day, one in a riverbed, one in the hills and the third near some houses. Two had partially or wholly discharged their TNT, causing the casings to split, and splattering the surrounding area with radioactive material. More than 1,000 men from Defense Department radiological units, wearing face masks and protective suits, spent the next three weeks shoveling up the 1,400 tons of contaminated vegetation and soil and packing it in 4,879 fifty-five-gallon drums for shipment to special disposal grounds in the U.S. The fourth bomb was nowhere to be seen. Like the surviving B-52 crew members, it had fallen into the Mediterranean, and it took a U.S. Navy search mission of 33 ships, four submersibles, 120 frogmen and more than 3,000 sailors two months to find it. The 5,000-pound, 10-foot-long bomb was eventually located five miles off the coast and 2,500 feet down. Each attempt to raise it seemed to drive it farther down. Finally, on April 7, it was retrieved by the U.S. Navy recovery force, using an experimental unmanned torpedo-retrieving apparatus called CURV (Cable-Controlled Underwater Research Vehicle) operated from the deck of a ship.

Not surprisingly, public anxiety about nuclear weapons continued to grow as U.S. and Soviet technology raced ahead. The new ingredients in SAC's arsenal—introduced between 1958 and 1962—were intercontinental ballistic missiles, which could find their targets by means of self-contained electronic or radar-directed navigation systems. Not only were both SAC and its Soviet counterpart building silos from which to lob huge weapons-bearing rockets at each other, they had also developed a variety of smaller missiles designed to be launched from airplanes. One jet-propelled air-to-ground missile, North American's Hound Dog, was able to deliver a one-megaton nuclear warhead; B-52 G and H models could carry a pair of Hound Dogs mounted in pods under the wings. When fired, the Hound Dog could travel at more than twice the speed of sound to a target 100 miles distant, or cruise at a higher altitude to a target 700 miles away, guided by its own jamproof computers. It could be released at any altitude the bomber commander chose, from 55,000 feet down to treetop level, and could even leap over ridges to destroy an enemy missile silo or radar site.

While air-to-ground missiles such as the Hound Dog could help a SAC jet blast its way through an enemy's defenses, other types of guided rocketry made the bombers increasingly vulnerable. Both the Soviet Union and the United States had developed a murderous stockpile of weapons that could home in by electronic or heat-seeking means on an enemy jet. Some, like the Russian SAMs, were surface-to-air missiles launched from the ground; others were carried under the wings of jet interceptors such as the Convair F-102 Delta Dagger and the Soviet MiG-21. The Sidewinder, developed by Ford Aerospace / Raytheon, was a heat seeker, and in 1961 it brought sudden tragedy to

At Loring Air Force Base in Maine, a B-52 wing's lumbering ordnance vehicles carry the bombers' deadly nuclear cargo to the flight line during a 1961 practice alert. All SAC bases are periodically subjected to surprise Operational Readiness Inspections in which evaluators grade each unit's performance under simulated combat conditions.

The swing-wing, supersonic B-1 bomber, seen here in a test flight over California, can fly to the Soviet Union and back without refueling. Its terrain-following radar enables it to fly a few hundred feet above the ground, a feature that would help it escape enemy interceptors in the event of war.

A swing-wing design like the B-1, the twin-engined Soviet Tupolev 22m is the most formidable offensive aircraft in the Red Air Force. Code-named "Backfire" by NATO, the plane has a top speed estimated at Mach 2 and can carry up to 12 tons of missiles or bombs; it has a shorter range than the B-1, however, and would require in-flight refueling to reach the continental U.S.

the crew of a B-52 on a SAC training flight over New Mexico.

The B-52 had taken off from Biggs Air Force Base, near El Paso, Texas, to radar-bomb various American cities. As part of the training exercise it carried a crew of eight, two more than its normal complement: pilot and copilot; two navigators; an electronic-warfare officer, who controlled the black boxes that would be used in a real war to jam enemy radar; an air-electronics officer, whose job was to monitor enemy electronic equipment; a crew chief in charge of maintaining the bomber's complicated flight systems; and in his own compartment in the rear, a tail gunner who wielded one radar-directed 20-millimeter cannon.

To add realism to an otherwise routine exercise, the bomber was to be intercepted by "enemy" fighters somewhere over the desert. The fighters were North American F-100 Super Sabres, descendants of the F-86 Sabre and the world's first operational supersonic jets. They would be flown by veteran pilots of the Air National Guard stationed at Kirtland in New Mexico, and each would carry live ammunition: 20-millimeter shells for four nose-mounted cannon, and a pair of Sidewinders slung under the wings. Neither the cannon nor the missiles would be able to fire, of course; a system of electronic safety devices would hold them in check, and all hits would be scored by radar.

As the big bomber streaked over the desert, almost seven miles up and at nearly 10 miles a minute, the aircraft commander, Captain Don Blodgett, called over the intercom to Sergeant Ray Singleton in the tail: "Tail gunner, this is AC."

"AC, this is tail gunner, go ahead."

"Ray, those National Guard planes are scheduled to make some passes at us pretty soon. Keep your eyes open for them."

"Roger, sir."

Not many minutes later, Singleton spotted the contrails of two F-100s. They streaked toward him on a simulated missile attack and then swept by overhead, almost too fast to catch in his gun sight.

Among the fighter pilots, First Lieutenant James Van Sycoc was leading what seemed to be a perfect mission. A 10-year veteran with more than 1,000 hours in jet fighters, he had honed his technique to perfection. Ground control had vectored him in toward the bomber with routine ease. Before moving in he had double-checked the safety switches and circuit breakers that muzzled the firing mechanisms on his cannon and missiles; they were all in "safe" positions. His first pass had netted him a radar "kill," and he circled back for a second run. Glancing at his fuel gauge and finding the indicator low, he called back to his wingman, "Okay, one more run and then we'll go home."

As Van Sycoc dived in on the bomber's tail for the next pass he felt his plane give a slight jerk. A long, cigar-shaped object streaked forward. The impossible had in fact happened. Stunned, then frantic with horror, Van Sycoc jabbed the transmit button on his radio. "Look out!" he cried. "One of my missiles has fired!"

But there was nothing to be done. With dreadful finality the Sidewinder nosed out the hot exhaust gases gushing from the B-52's left wing and connected. There was an intense orange flash and black smoke as the twin engines exploded. The bomber took a violent roll to the left and began twisting crazily out of the sky.

Five crewmen were able to bail out, and landed in the wilderness of nearby Mount Taylor. The three others—the air-electronics officer and the two navigators—were trapped inside; they crashed into the mountain in a blaze of jet fuel and incandescent metal.

Search planes and rescue helicopters found pilot Blodgett, tail gunner Singleton and electronic-warfare officer Captain George Jackson. All three were badly injured: Blodgett had a fractured pelvis, Jackson a broken spine, and Singleton had been terribly burned.

As the search continued for the other men, the weather turned nasty. It was early April, and a spring blizzard gusted in with freezing, 70-mile-per-hour winds and heavy snow. The storm howled all night and throughout the following day. On April 9, when the sky had cleared and the rescue flights resumed, someone noticed a flash of light from the ground. It was Sergeant Manuel Mieras, the crew chief, who was signaling with a hand mirror from his survival kit; he had broken a leg but was otherwise uninjured. Then the searchers found Captain Ray Obel, the copilot, who had landed in a cactus patch and was suffering from lacerations, cold and exposure.

What human error or mechanical quirk had sent an eight-million-dollar jet bomber into oblivion? Very little, it turned out. Van Sycoc was absolved of blame. All his safety controls were in the proper position, as examination later revealed. Furthermore, his two missiles had been programed to fire in a certain sequence, and the second missile was the one that had let go—a theoretical impossibility. So the engineers at Albuquerque stripped down the firing circuits and located the trouble: A tiny drop of moisture had shorted out a circuit, causing the missile to release. The Sidewinder had, in effect, fired itself.

The most extraordinary thing about such mishaps was their rarity. In spite of all the thousands of missions SAC had flown in the decades since World War II, and all the millions of hours spent in training and in airborne alerts, few lives had been lost and little damage done. No chance explosion of a bomb had plunged the world into nuclear war. And time and again, in their role as the United States' main deterrent force, the great SAC jets had turned the world away from open conflict. Never in history had one nation enjoyed such an enormous measure of military superiority as the U.S. and yet used it—not for its own aggrandizement—but purely to keep others from using their own strength to hostile ends.

One of the most striking demonstrations of SAC's deterrent powers occurred over the Caribbean in the autumn of 1962. It was a time of acute international tension. The Soviet Union had been building an

In this photograph of the Cuban countryside, taken in 1962 by a U-2 reconnaissance plane, geometric shapes scattered among the trees betray an alarming presence. Eight medium-range missiles (1) capable of hitting U.S. cities rest on trailers next to launchers (2), while fuel trucks (3) stand nearby. A cluster of tents (4) houses Russian crews manning the site.

enormous stockpile of nuclear warheads, along with the rockets to deliver them. None of these could yet reach the U.S. from Soviet territory, but they had been potent enough to loft a succession of cosmonauts into orbit around the earth. The year before, the Russians had exploded a thermonuclear bomb of 58 megatons—the largest nuclear test ever. There was trouble in Berlin, where the Russians were building a wall to seal off their sector of the city that had been divided among the Allies after World War II. Against this backdrop of mounting unrest and belligerence General Thomas S. Power, who had succeeded LeMay as SAC commander in chief in a normal rotation of duties in July 1957, put one third of SAC's bombers on ground alert and increased the number of bombers patrolling the air.

Part of SAC's task at this time was to fly photoreconnaissance missions over Cuba and monitor Russian shipments of arms to the Communist regime of Fidel Castro. Most of the weapons were nonstrategic—rifles and machine guns, personnel carriers, antiaircraft guns and the like. Then, in late summer of 1962, the arms freighters began arriving in unprecedented numbers and unloading crates of SAMs. Even these posed no immediate danger to the U.S.; SAMs are designed primarily to knock down attacking aircraft. But there was much concern that larger missiles would follow—medium- and long-range rockets that could rain down nuclear terror upon American cities. And so still more reconnaissance flights were ordered.

SAC's favored aircraft for the Cuban missions was a long, gray single-seater of striking elegance, the Lockheed U-2, which had been developed specifically for reconnaissance flights over the Soviet Union. With a single turbine and an 80-foot wingspan, it operated in the upper atmosphere as a combination jet and glider. It could fly undetected at an astonishing 80,000 feet, higher than any other aircraft of its day and well above most antiaircraft systems. Only the newest type of Soviet rocket could come close to it; one of these had in fact shot down a U-2 piloted by Francis Gary Powers of the Central Intelligence Agency on a photographic mission over the Soviet Union two years earlier—an incident that had contributed substantially to the present state of world tension.

As the SAC U-2s swept over Cuba, 15 miles up and with their high-resolution cameras rolling, they recorded the alarming extent of the Soviet build-up. The Russians were installing dozens of SAMs in launching sites around the island. They were also uncrating worrisome numbers of MiG fighters and twin-engined Ilyushin 28 medium bombers.

Then on October 14, U-2 pilots Major Rudolph Anderson Jr. and Major Richard S. Heyser returned from photographing a SAM site at San Cristobal with the evidence everyone was dreading. There on the prints, poking out from under a camouflage tent, was the long, slick cylinder of a large rocket, while nearby could be seen several tank trucks for liquid-oxygen propellant. "Let's be clear about what we're looking at," said America's senior photo interpreter, Arthur C. Lundahl. "It's a medium-range ballistic missile site."

Four U.S. Navy supersonic F-8 fighters streak past ships departing the American base at Guantanamo Bay during the Cuban missile crisis of 1962. Both planes and ships were on the alert for vessels transporting Soviet military matériel to Cuba.

The pictures were rushed to the White House and displayed before President Kennedy. He studied them, listened to Lundahl's diagnosis and made up his mind. Russia could not be allowed to deploy strategic missiles within shooting distance of the U.S. And so, on Kennedy's orders, U.S. armed forces made ready to go to war. The Navy steamed into the Caribbean to set up a blockade, with orders to stop, search and turn back all Soviet transports. Marines and paratroopers started drilling for a landing on Cuba itself. And every unit in SAC was placed on ground alert. Scores of B-47s and B-52s were sent cruising overhead on 24-hour missions.

As the crisis deepened, the surveillance flights continued. When Admiral George W. Anderson Jr., an aviator himself and Chief of Naval Operations, expounded on the complexity of locating and tracking all the Soviet ships, General LeMay, who was now Air Force Chief of Staff, reassured him. "Give us four hours and we'll find every ship on the Atlantic Ocean," he said, and he began flooding the Navy Department with a deluge of reconnaissance photographs and reports giving the type, name, speed and direction of each vessel sighted. To backstop the U-2s, LeMay sent in McDonnell RF-101 Voodoo supersonic jets from the Tactical Air Command. The jets could fly in low under the Russians' radar screen for reconnaissance work; one Voodoo skimmed so close over its target that it almost hit a volleyball being tossed by a Russian technician during a game.

It was an impressive display of muscle flexing. During the crisis SAC's bombers, tankers and U-2s flew 2,088 sorties, logging 48,532 hours of flying time and covering more than 20 million air miles. And in that period there were only five casualties. On October 27 an RB-47 crashed on takeoff from Kindley Air Force Base in Bermuda, killing all four crew members. And that same day Major Anderson, flying yet another U-2 mission over the Cuban sites, was brought down in flames by a Russian SAM. Then the very next day the Soviets backed down. Faced with the Navy's interdiction, and under the implied threat of SAC's nuclear arsenal, they started dismantling their missiles and shipping them home. The crisis evaporated as quickly as it had arisen.

In the 1970s and early 1980s, much of SAC's nuclear deterrent was shifted to its own long-range missiles, nested in silos on land. The B-47s had been phased out. But the great B-52s, the BUFFS, kept flying. Some were heavily modified, with improved weapons systems and performance. Some of the planes were old enough to be flown by the sons of their original pilots. The SAC training continued, tough as always, along with the grueling alerts and the 24-hour missions with nuclear warheads. The hope remained, passionate as ever, that they would never be used. And while the bombers still maintained their patrols, they were sometimes diverted to other tasks. Like their predecessor B-29s in Korea, many were sent into combat with conventional bombs, to fight a long, hot war in another small Asian country few Americans had even heard of before the shooting started.

The workhorse jets of the Vietnam conflict

During the Vietnam War, American pilots fought what one of them called "the grimmest contest yet conceived between sophisticated air and ground machinery and people." That deadly contest embraced several kinds of missions: high-level bombing sorties to destroy bridges and rail lines, low-level strikes to knock out missiles and gun emplacements, treetop-level strafing runs to support ground troops and air-to-air dogfights against enemy jets.

To meet these varied demands, virtually every type of jet in Air Force and Navy inventories was brought to bear against the Viet Cong and the North Vietnamese.

The workhorse jets of the air war in Vietnam were the F-100 fighter-bomber *(right),* widely used for ground-support missions in the South; the rugged and reliable A-4 Skyhawk *(below);* the F-105 fighter-bomber, which carried out 75 per cent of the strikes against the North between 1965 and 1969; the Grumman A-6 Intruder, whose sophisticated "black-box" electronics made it America's best all-weather fighter-bomber; and the F-4 Phantom, the most versatile combat jet in the American arsenal.

These five planes are illustrated on the following pages, as are the Soviet-built MiG-21—their frequent aerial foe and the most widely deployed combat jet in the world in the 1970s—and the F-5, the most sophisticated plane employed by South Vietnam's Air Force.

The aircraft on facing pages are drawn in scale, and all are shown with appropriate markings and insignia; the year in which each model became operational is given in parentheses.

NORTH AMERICAN F-100D SUPER SABRE (1954)
The Super Sabre was the world's first supersonic fighter, with a top speed of 910 mph, and the first plane with a structure incorporating heat-resistant titanium alloys. The F-100 was armed with four 20-mm. internal cannon, two 500-pound bombs attached to inboard wing racks and two larger napalm bombs carried on outboard racks. The jet had a 1,060-mile range that could be extended via in-flight refueling through the boom on its right wing.

MCDONNELL DOUGLAS A-4E SKYHAWK (1956)
The Skyhawk, nicknamed the Scooter by carrier-based Navy pilots because of its nimble performance, is shown with its weapons expended and its arresting hook, wing flaps and slats down for landing. Powered by a Pratt & Whitney J52-P-6A engine that delivered 8,500 pounds of thrust, the five-ton delta-winged jet could fly at 685 mph and carry nearly its own weight in bombs and rockets. The pod under its belly is a 300-gallon external fuel tank.

MIG-21PF (1959)
The MiG-21, here bearing markings of the North Vietnamese Air Force, was designed immediately following the Korean War to meet Soviet needs for a supersonic day interceptor. The delta-winged jet had a top speed of 1,285 mph and carried two Atoll air-to-air heat-seeking missiles. Through the 1970s, various versions of the MiG-21 were employed by the air forces of 34 nations.

REPUBLIC F-105D THUNDERCHIEF (1958)
The F-105D, at the time the world's heaviest single-seat jet at 50,000 pounds fully loaded, is shown here carrying six 750-pound bombs under the fuselage and electronic-countermeasure pods on each wing to confuse enemy missile-tracking and guidance radars. The plane had a top speed of 1,390 mph and carried an internal 20-mm. Vulcan cannon that fired an awesome 6,000 rounds per minute.

MCDONNELL DOUGLAS F-4D PHANTOM II (1961)
Pilots called the twin-engined Phantom "brutishly ugly," but lauded its exceptional performance. The plane, which had a top speed of 1,500 mph, was used in Vietnam as an air-superiority fighter and for both high- and low-level bombing runs. The aircraft shown here is equipped with two Sparrow air-to-air missiles. The large centerline pod is a laser target illuminator used to guide bombs dropped by other planes.

GRUMMAN A-6A INTRUDER (1963)
With a top speed of only 625 mph, the U.S. Navy's A-6 relied on sophisticated radar, navigation and attack systems to complete its mission in any kind of weather. It was armed with thirty 500-pound bombs for pinpoint bombing—at which the two-man craft excelled. The periscopic boom on the nose was used for in-flight refueling.

NORTHROP F-5A (1964)
Dubbed the "Freedom Fighter," the F-5A was designed to give pro-American air forces an inexpensive jet fighter that would be easy to fly and maintain. The twin-engined craft, which had a top speed of 925 mph, is seen here in the markings of the South Vietnamese Air Force, which first took delivery of the plane in 1967. It was armed with two 20-mm. nose cannon and two 750-pound bombs under each wing.

4

The war of a million sorties

Red strips of canvas fluttered like ribbons from the undersides of two Republic F-105 Thunderchiefs as they taxied to the end of the runway at Korat Air Base, Thailand, and halted, engines at idle. A huge, heavy aircraft for a single-seater—pilots called it the Thud—the F-105 was, in the mid-1960s, the U.S. Air Force's best fighter-bomber. Armorers ducked agilely beneath the planes, plucking off the strips, then stood displaying them to the pilots. At the end of each strip dangled a safety pin that had until that moment disarmed the craft's bombs or missiles; now they were ready for action.

The pilots acknowledged the armorers' signals, taxied onto the runway, pushed their throttles forward and just after noon on April 3, 1965, thundered aloft. Within minutes, they were joined by the rest of their squadron for the two-hour flight across the mountains of Laos—a region of craggy, rainswept beauty, abrupt river chasms and jungle valleys—to the broad coastal deltas of North Vietnam.

In command of the lead formation was Robinson Risner, the Korean War ace who had once chased a MiG between hangars at a Communist airfield and driven it straight into the ground. Now a lieutenant colonel, Risner was in the vanguard of the largest air strike against North Vietnam since raids had commenced the preceding month.

The strike had been carefully planned. Risner's squadron was to be joined by other Thuds from Takhli Air Base, also in Thailand, bringing the total of F-105s to 46. Four F-100 Super Sabres from South Vietnam would fly MiGCAP (MiG Combat Air Patrol), their duty to shoot down any North Vietnamese MiGs that might appear. Other F-100s, 17 of them, were to fly weather reconnaissance, attack antiaircraft batteries that threatened the fighter-bombers, or cover the rescue of any pilot who might be shot down. Ten KC-135 tankers would orbit over Laos to refuel the strike force on its way in. And a pair of RF-101 Voodoos would photograph the damage. The target of this mighty fleet, 79 planes in all, was a 540-foot railroad-and-highway bridge—known as the Dragon's Jaw—that spanned the Song Ma at Thanh Hoa.

Success depended on perfect timing. The Thud squadrons rendezvoused on schedule with the tankers, then angled east across the North Vietnamese border to a point about three minutes' flying time south of the Thanh Hoa Bridge. Here was the so-called IP, or Initial Point, the start of the bomb run on the target. Already columns of smoke were rising to mingle with the afternoon haze—the work of the F-100s, which

Captain Harry J. Eckes, an F-4 Phantom pilot with the 390th Tactical Fighter Wing in Vietnam, prepares for a late-afternoon takeoff from Danang in 1966. Normally, Air Force pilots flew a tour of one year or 100 missions before being rotated; this was Eckes' 115th combat mission.

had flown up the Vietnamese coast and were still pounding the enemy's antiaircraft batteries with rocket fire.

Risner headed north toward the smoke, spotted the Dragon's Jaw and rolled in on the bridge from 17,000 feet. Under each wing he carried a 250-pound radio-guided Bullpup, then the Air Force's standard air-to-ground missile. Steered manually by radio signals from the attack plane, Bullpups had proved capable of pinpoint accuracy.

Cotton-ball puffs from the dozen or so flak batteries still operating dotted the sky. Risner dived down through the detonating shells, and at 12,000 feet he launched his first Bullpup. Then he circled once and unleashed his second missile.

Just as the missile reached its target, Risner's plane gave a violent lurch; a fragment from a 37-millimeter antiaircraft shell had hit his fuselage. Smoke and fumes began seeping into the cockpit. Struggling to retain control of the F-105, Risner headed south out of the battle. Gradually, the smoke cleared from his cockpit, allowing him to land his damaged Thud at the sprawling air base at Danang in South Vietnam.

Meanwhile, the rest of the strike force swept over the Dragon's Jaw. The next 15 planes launched their Bullpups, and the remaining 30 pounded the bridge with conventional 750-pound bombs, then followed the others back to Thailand. They left behind two aircraft, an F-100 that had helped to suppress flak and an RF-101; both had taken direct hits and crashed.

The remaining RF-101 returned with photographs of the strike, and what they showed was not encouraging. Opened just the year before, the Dragon's Jaw had been built to withstand heavy bombardment. The 250-pound Bullpups, for all their uncanny precision, had not even dented it. The 750-pound bombs, dropped from as low as 3,600 feet for maximum accuracy, had cratered the roadway and bent part of the superstructure, but the bridge remained standing. The damage would be easy to repair. Again and again, U.S. jets would pound the Dragon's Jaw with explosives, to equally little effect, until the bridge came to represent all the frustrations of a war that seemed to run on forever.

The events that led to the strike against the Dragon's Jaw seemed to have had no clear beginning. Ever since the early 1950s a small group of U.S. military advisers had been based in Saigon to train the fledgling armed forces of South Vietnam and to help them subdue the bands of Communist-supported Viet Cong guerrillas operating in the countryside. The Americans, though they carried weapons, were under orders not to use them except in self-defense. But the line between defense and offense can be indistinct, and with the guerrillas ambushing convoys and raiding military posts, the Americans found themselves shooting more and more often. By the autumn of 1961 three U.S. Army helicopter companies were buzzing the jungles around Saigon in search of Viet Cong encampments, and a clandestine U.S. Air Force Air Commando unit was flying ground-attack missions in armed T-28 trainers that bore South Vietnamese insignia. All the while, American planners were taking a long, hard look across the 17th Parallel at Communist North Vietnam, from which the guerrillas' food and munitions flowed.

For the next three years the shadow war continued, all but ignored by the American public. Then on August 2, 1964, it lurched into the open. A U.S. Navy destroyer, the *Maddox,* was cruising in the Gulf of Tonkin with the dual purpose of sniffing out North Vietnam's radar defenses and of observing a raid on some small North Vietnamese naval bases by South Vietnamese Navy commandos. Suddenly, three high-speed PT boats swung out from the coast and launched torpedoes at the *Maddox.* The torpedoes missed, but the *Maddox* opened fire, damaging one of the boats. Two nights later, another small force unsuccessfully attacked the *C. Turner Joy,* sent to reinforce the *Maddox* after the first attack.

It was scarcely Pearl Harbor, but President Lyndon Johnson felt that letting this Gulf of Tonkin Incident, as it came to be known, pass unanswered would be interpreted as American weakness by North Vietnam. Within 12 hours he sent Navy jets from the carriers *Ticonderoga* and *Constellation* on a retaliatory strike against the PT bases at Vinh; for good measure, the jets hit an oil depot nearby. Then, on August 7, Congress passed a resolution granting Johnson a virtual carte blanche to take the United States into the War. Before the decade was out, more

F-105 fighter-bombers, parked between sandbag revetments for protection against rocket and mortar attack, crowd the flight line at Danang air base in South Vietnam. Danang—with its 10,000-foot runway—was a major jumping-off point for air strikes against the North.

than half a million American troops would be fighting in South Vietnam. Virtually every type of American jet would be streaking into battle from bases in Vietnam, Thailand and Guam. Even SAC's B-52s, modified to carry 100 or more bombs in their bomb bays and under their wings, would take part. Altogether, U.S. jets would fly more than a million attack sorties before the War was over. Some of the missions would be dispatched in support of the ground troops in the South; others would attempt to cripple the Communists by striking supply routes in Laos and Cambodia, Vietnam's neighbors to the west. But the most dangerous raids, the exacting missions that made heroes of the men who flew them, were aimed at North Vietnam.

The strikes against the North were part of a bombing campaign, called Operation *Rolling Thunder,* directed against railroads, highways and military installations. The first raid, on March 2, 1965, had smashed an ammunition dump just above the 17th Parallel, the dividing line between the two Vietnams. From there the strikes rumbled progressively northward, and in April they reached the Dragon's Jaw.

The very afternoon that Colonel Risner landed his shot-up F-105 safely at Danang, he hopped a flight back to Korat and rejoined his squadron. The next morning, he and his men were off to attack the bridge again. This time 48 F-105s took off from Thailand, all loaded with 750-pound bombs. Once again the strike force rolled in toward the Dragon's Jaw behind a sweep of F-100s. The flak was worse than on the preceding day; during the night, the North Vietnamese had moved in additional batteries. The first F-105 to bomb the target caught a 37-millimeter shell and exploded in mid-air. Its pilot, Captain Carlyle Harris, bailed out into a paddy and was captured.

Then, as the last flight of F-105s circled the IP, awaiting their turn to attack the bridge, a new threat screamed in from overhead. Four North Vietnamese MiG-17s—improved versions of the Korean War-vintage MiG-15—emerged through the haze. Unnoticed by the F-100 pilots flying MiGCAP, the Communist jets attacked the bomb-laden F-105s from behind, cannon blazing. It was the first MiG attack of the War, and it was over in seconds. The Thunderchiefs were easy targets. Taken completely by surprise, they had no opportunity to evade the attack. A torrent of cannon fire splashed across two of the Thuds, which crashed. A grim new dimension had been added to the War.

More than 300 bombs, three fourths of the number dropped that day, had exploded against the bridge, blowing away minor beams and large chunks of concrete. But the Dragon's Jaw still spanned the river, and in a month it would again be carrying supplies south. By mid-June the Navy had taken over the task of pummeling the Dragon's Jaw, while the Air Force F-105s intruded farther north—even beyond Hanoi—to blast rail yards, bridges and thatch-roofed military barracks.

With each new strike, the enemy's defenses grew more murderous. Not a week passed without the loss of at least one American plane. If the pilot attacked at an altitude below 5,000 feet, he would run head on into

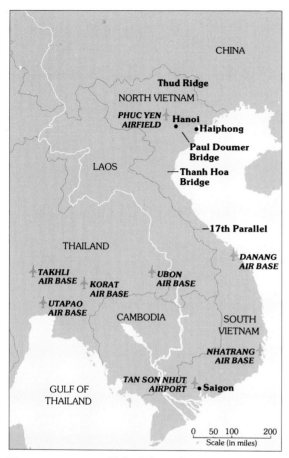

The most important U.S. air bases in South Vietnam and Thailand, as well as major North Vietnamese targets, can be seen on this map of Southeast Asia. Between 1966 and 1973, U.S. pilots—operating from these bases, the island of Guam and aircraft carriers—flew more than 328,000 sorties against the North.

a tempest of machine-gun and light-cannon fire from the ground; a lucky hit could sever electrical circuits or hydraulic lines and send the plane spinning out of control. Between 5,000 feet and 25,000 feet, the main hazard was heavy-caliber cannon fire. The guns fired explosive shells as big as 100 millimeters in diameter, and a near miss could be as fatal as a direct hit. Many of the guns were aimed by radar that could judge the speed, altitude and range of an approaching jet with decimal-point accuracy. Above 2,000 feet—and all the way up to 59,000 feet, far higher than a fully laden Thud could fly—there was another menace, the SA-2 guided missile. Resembling nothing so much as a flying telephone pole, the SA-2 was steered by radar instructions from the ground, and it could vault upward at double the speed of sound to blast a plane from the sky. And at almost any altitude there were MiGs—and not just MiG-17s, but a new generation of MiG-19 and MiG-21 interceptors. All of them could be vectored in for a kill by radar controllers.

One F-105 pilot, Colonel Jack Broughton of the 355th Tactical Fighter Wing at Takhli, told what it was like: "If you dragged your force in too low, the ground fire got them. If you brought them in too high, where the MiG was in his preferred envelope, he could force you to lighten your aircraft for better performance by jettisoning your bombs. If you flew straight and level, either in the clouds or in the clear, the SAM could get you. If you flew on top of an undercast, you couldn't see SAM when he launched, and he most probably would gobble you up."

American pilots flew into this hornet's nest in some of the world's most advanced jets. Since Korea, the fighting jet had gained enormously in speed, size and sophistication. Beginning with the North American F-100, the Air Force commissioned the so-called Century Series fighters, each one supersonic and each a technological breakthrough.

The F-100, for example, was the first jet to exceed the speed of sound in level flight. The McDonnell F-101 set a speed record in 1957 of 1,207 miles per hour and could fly 1,900 miles without refueling. Convair's F-102 Delta Dagger, a high-altitude interceptor, was a marvel of aerodynamics: Its pinched-in "Coke-bottle" waist reduced drag, and a delta-shaped wing boosted lift and maneuverability. Its only weapons were missiles guided by the plane's computerized fire-control devices. Yet another advance came with Lockheed's F-104 Starfighter, the world's first Mach 2 combat aircraft. Designed as an interceptor, it had thin, stubby wings on a sharply pointed fuselage. The F-104 looked more like a missile than an airplane, and with a top speed of 1,450 miles per hour and a climb rate of 40,000 feet a minute, it behaved like one. Then came the F-105 and even an F-106, a hotter version of the F-102.

Though F-100s, F-102s and F-104s all served in Vietnam, none played as large a role in the air war north of the 17th Parallel as the Thunderchief. The fastest plane at low altitudes in Vietnam—it could exceed Mach 1 at sea level—the F-105 flew 75 per cent of the air strikes directed against the North. The jet was 64 feet long and had a 35-foot wingspan. Powered by a Pratt & Whitney J-75 engine that developed

The pilot of a TF-102 interceptor, his helmet and face mask silhouetted against Vietnam's landscape, banks in formation with two F-100 fighter-bombers.

26,500 pounds of thrust, it had been planned as a nuclear-weapons carrier, designed to streak in low, zoom up and lob a small atomic bomb toward its target. But in Vietnam it was pressed into service as a delivery truck for conventional bombs. It could carry seven tons of explosives.

The Thud proved extraordinarily tough. One F-105 came home safely after a heat-seeking missile exploded against the tailpipe, causing damage that would have been fatal to a less sturdily built aircraft. After flying a few missions in it, many a pilot came to revere the plane. "A startling fact became apparent," recalled Colonel Broughton. "The Thud was getting to North Vietnam as nothing else could. Nobody could keep up with the Thud as it flew at high speed on the deck, at treetop level. Nobody could carry that load and penetrate those defenses except the Thud. It was the old Thud that, day after day, every day, lunged into that mess, outdueled the opposition, put the bombs on the target and dashed back to strike again."

The Navy had its own favorites. Among them was Douglas Aircraft Company's single-seat A-4 Skyhawk, an attack bomber renowned for its light weight, fuel efficiency and ease of maintenance. As the Navy's principal workhorse, the Skyhawk flew most of the carrier-based daytime missions along the North Vietnamese coast—including 208 sorties against the Dragon's Jaw.

A world away in computerized sophistication was the Navy's two-seat, all-weather attack aircraft, the Grumman A-6 Intruder. It was packed with electronic black boxes, and this complexity made the jet both expensive and difficult to maintain. But for most of the War, it was the only aircraft in Vietnam that could reliably hit a target with pinpoint accuracy during the rainy season and in darkness. In one memorable night assault, two Intruders struck a power station near Haiphong with just 13 bombs apiece. All fell within the perimeter fence of the installation, virtually obliterating the plant. An earlier daytime strike by 100 less specialized aircraft had caused only superficial damage.

The Navy had a new fighter, too: the all-weather F-4 Phantom. Designed by McDonnell as an interceptor to protect U.S. carriers from air attack, the Phantom could be armed with four radar-guided Sparrows and an equal number of heat-seeking Sidewinder air-to-air missiles; early models had no guns. Or it could carry up to eight tons of bombs. Its computerized radar-tracking and fire-control systems were operated from the seat behind the pilot by a Radar Intercept Officer known as a GIB, for "guy in back." The Navy ordered up huge numbers of these versatile craft and began flying the jet from carriers in the Gulf of Tonkin in 1964. The Air Force, recognizing the Phantom for the remarkable warplane that it was, followed suit. The first USAF F-4s arrived in the war zone just as *Rolling Thunder* commenced.

At that time, there were hundreds of jet fighters within striking distance of North Vietnam. Yet there was very little to bomb. Years before the F-105s and F-100s began their work above the 17th Parallel, the gener-

Tracked by an F-105 Thunderchief returning from a bombing raid northeast of Hanoi, a MiG-17 takes a fatal hit on the wing, then erupts in flames in this 1967 gun-camera sequence. The U.S. fighter-bomber pilot aimed his 20-mm. cannon slightly to the right of his prey in order to anticipate the MiG's flight path.

als in Washington had attempted to catalogue targets in Vietnam, Laos and Cambodia. They had drawn a blank. "Indochina," declared the Joint Chiefs of Staff in a 1954 report, "is devoid of decisive military targets." Then, in a reassessment undertaken just months before the Gulf of Tonkin Incident in 1964, the Joint Chiefs came up with a list of 94 strategic targets in North Vietnam—mostly roads, bridges, rail yards, storage depots and the like. The American commanders, convinced that a quick, preemptive strike against all 94 might persuade the Communists to make peace right then, urged that course; but it was not taken. President Johnson, unwilling to risk provoking the Chinese or the Russians, moved instead with utmost caution.

Air strikes were severely restricted in scope, and each mission was ordered individually from Washington. Bombing was forbidden within 25 miles of the Chinese border, and within 10 miles of Hanoi and four miles of Haiphong. The North Vietnamese quickly figured out the constraints on American fliers. They knew, for example, that a flak battery set up on a river dam was inviolable. If a bomb were to destroy the dam, towns and fields would be flooded, something the Americans naturally wanted to avoid. The Vietnamese knew, too, that there could be no attacks on MiG airfields, because the Americans believed Russian technicians were there. In the early months of *Rolling Thunder* the Americans were not to hit any SAM site unless it fired a missile at them.

And woe to any pilot who defied these bans. Colonel Broughton tells of one flier who, heading back from a strike up north in his Thud, noticed an unfinished SAM site. Under the rules, the only action he could take was to report its location. But some antiaircraft guns were already in place, and as he flew over they lofted shells at him. So he circled back and raked the guns with his 20-millimeter cannon. "He shot up a storm," Broughton said. "He blew up construction gear that burst into flame. He ripped open SAM fire-control gear." And he ignited some of the missiles, which "raced about the area like fiery snakes, gone wild and chasing their masters." The next day a stream of telephone calls rippled down the chain of command; he was to be grounded and hauled before a court-martial. But the pilot had already taken off on his next mission, from which he did not return.

Shortly after this incident, as SAMs began to fire regularly at American jets, the taboo was lifted. But the missiles remained a threat, even after each jet was fitted with a hurriedly designed electronic sensor that picked up the signals from enemy radar searching for approaching aircraft. If the radar locked onto a Phantom or a Thud and began tracking, a warning light flashed in the cockpit and the sensor emitted a loud burst of static, like the sound of a rattlesnake about to strike. At this alert, a pilot could head for the deck, braving the inevitable flak and machine-gun fire. Or he could wait until the SAM was launched and then try to outmaneuver the missile as it streaked toward him.

The second choice demanded steel nerves and adroit stickwork. "The trick," said Colonel Robin Olds, commander of the 8th Tactical

Fighter Wing at Ubon Air Base in Thailand, "is seeing the launch. You can see the steam. The SAM goes straight up, turns more level, then the booster drops off." Timing was critical. "If you dodge too fast," Olds continued, "it will turn and catch you; if you wait too late it will explode near enough to get you. What you do at the right moment is poke your nose down, go down as hard as you can, and once it follows you down, you go up as hard as you can. It can't follow that and goes under."

Other defenses depended on specially outfitted aircraft. SAM radars could be jammed by powerful transmitters carried in under-the-wing pods by Thuds and Phantoms or packed by the ton into larger aircraft such as the twin-engined Douglas EB-66 jet bomber. This plane could orbit at a safe distance and wrap an entire battlefield with signals that blanked out whole segments of enemy radar screens.

But the best defense was to silence the radars. This hazardous task fell to the so-called Wild Weasels—F-100s at first, then Thuds and eventually F-4s—which were equipped with an array of weapons including Shrike missiles that homed in on the enemy radar beam. The Wild Weasels would fly in ahead of the main strike force to provoke the SAMs. At the rattlesnake buzz indicating a radar lock, the Wild Weasel pilot loosed a Shrike. At the end of its flight, the missile blew up the radar. SAM crews soon learned to operate their radar intermittently—just long enough at any one time to track the American plane and turn the encounter into a duel that the Weasel sometimes lost.

Ferocious SAM attacks were only one hazard; the Thuds and Phantoms also found themselves flying through skies sometimes swarming with fighters. Obsolescent MiG-17s, slow but exceptionally maneuverable at low altitude, posed a surprisingly serious threat to the United States' latest jets below 20,000 feet. The MiG-19, a supersonic aircraft with a top speed of 919 miles per hour and three heavy-hitting 30-millimeter cannon aimed by radar, also made a dangerous opponent. The trim, delta-winged MiG-21 could streak toward its quarry at Mach 2, outpacing a bomb-laden Phantom or an early-model Thud. And in a dogfight, it could outturn both, though it could not outclimb the F-4. Typically, a flight of MiGs would lie in wait at low altitudes, where they were difficult for U.S. MiGCAP pilots to detect. Then, as the American strike force rolled in toward its target, they would zoom from behind and attack the trailing two or three aircraft with a barrage of cannon fire or heat-seeking Atoll missiles, poor copies of the American Sidewinder.

By the end of 1966 the MiGs had become such a nuisance—they regularly forced pilots to jettison their bombs—that remedial action was clearly needed. It took the form of a classic fighter sweep. On January 2, 1967, a force of 56 Phantoms, led by Colonel Olds, headed north toward Hanoi. To entice the MiGs, Olds ordered his planes to fly in a typical strike formation, mimicking the customary mixed force of attack aircraft, Wild Weasels, radar jammers and reconnaissance planes.

The F-4s swept in from Laos and turned south along Thud Ridge, terrain so rugged that the enemy could mount few antiaircraft guns on it,

After leading one of the biggest air-to-air battles of the Vietnam War, Colonel Robin Olds (left) stands with fellow pilot Captain John Stone. Seven MiGs were shot down during the operation, prompting comedian Bob Hope, then touring Vietnam, to call the fliers "the largest distributors of MiG parts in the world."

toward Phuc Yen airfield, where most of North Vietnam's MiG-21s were based. Olds started swinging back and forth above a 7,000-foot overcast that shrouded the field, hoping to lure the MiGs up.

Soon enough they came popping out of the clouds. One fastened on Olds's flight, and his wingman turned to engage it. About a mile and a quarter ahead, and a little to the left, Olds spotted a second MiG. He told his back seater, First Lieutenant Charles Clifton, to lock the Phantom's radar onto it. Seconds later, Olds launched two Sparrow missiles in close succession. But he had come too near the target for the radar to continue tracking it, and both missiles missed.

Quickly, Olds switched to his Sidewinders. These heat-seeking missiles were effective at shorter range than the Sparrow. Before launch, the Sidewinder transmits a growling noise into the pilot's headset if it has sensed a heat source it can home in on. "I put the pipper on the MiG," Olds remembered, "as he was disappearing into the overcast, received an indistinct missile growl and fired." It missed. Olds had set off $24,000 worth of sophisticated fireworks—and had nothing to show for it.

Just ahead was another MiG. "I pulled sharp left," Olds recalled, "barrel rolled to the right, held my position above and behind the MiG." When Olds was within range he "completed the rolling maneuver and fell in behind and below the MiG-21 at his seven o'clock position."

The MiG clawed skyward, but to no avail. "I put my pipper on his tailpipe," Olds said, "received a perfect growl, squeezed the trigger once, then once again." The first missile did the job. It "went slightly down, then arced gracefully upward. Suddenly the MiG-21 erupted in a brilliant flash of orange flame. It then fell, twisting, corkscrewing, tumbling lazily toward the top of the clouds."

Olds had scored his first MiG kill, but Lieutenant Clifton received equal credit—the U.S. Air Force recognized the crucial role in air-to-air combat played by the Weapon Systems Officer, as the Air Force called the man riding in the back seat. Other pilots accounted for six more North Vietnamese fighters that day.

After this air battle, the largest so far in Vietnam, the MiGs became increasingly wary. In May, airfields were briefly taken off the list of prohibited targets and the Phantom pilots had the satisfaction of smashing 26 MiGs on the ground. In August, Thuds bearing 3,000-pound bombs blitzed the Paul Doumer Bridge near Hanoi. Once off limits because of its proximity to the capital, this all-important road-and-rail link to China and Haiphong was put out of commission for nearly two months, depriving North Vietnam of the 6,000 tons of supplies that could be carried across it each day.

To constrict the flow of troops and supplies into South Vietnam was, of course, the object of bombing the North. Yet none of the thousands upon thousands of tons of explosives dropped above the 17th Parallel seemed to have a lasting effect. Part of the reason lay in Washington's reluctance to escalate the air war, which allowed the North Vietnamese to compensate for the piecemeal damage to their supply lines. But equally important were the Communists' determination to build their strength in South Vietnam and the resilient network of supply routes they established. The Ho Chi Minh Trail, which paralleled South Vietnam in Laos and Cambodia, was actually a web of jungle roads and tracks. Bombing one route merely diverted traffic to another.

By the late autumn of 1967, the war in South Vietnam began to change character. Battles that would once have been fought by Viet Cong units composed mostly of South Vietnamese insurgents were now undertaken by North Vietnamese Army regulars, who had come south in division strength. For months, the Communists carefully husbanded their forces. Then on the 31st of January, 1968, as the celebration of the Buddhist New Year, Tet, commenced, masses of North Vietnamese troops charged across the 17th Parallel in a Korea-style offensive. Throughout South Vietnam, the Viet Cong and their north-

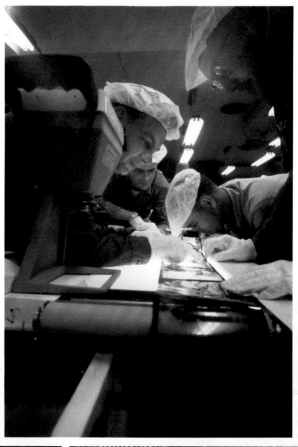

Air Force photo interpreters, wearing caps and gloves to keep dandruff or fingerprints from marring the film they examine, pore over aerial photographs at Saigon's Tan Son Nhut Airport. Picture experts processed and studied more than three million contact prints a month to pinpoint targets for American warplanes, including (from left): a ring of 57-mm. antiaircraft cannon guarding a bridge approach in the North, a SAM site, and two MiG-17s in a revetment at a field outside Hanoi.

ern allies launched major assaults against province and district capitals.

The timing and strength of the attack took U.S. and South Vietnamese forces by surprise, and initial reports of the battle were alarming. But the foe was now out in the open and vulnerable to the firepower that the Americans had assembled in Southeast Asia. In South Vietnam, a jet pilot rarely saw the enemy. Usually his aiming point was a puff of smoke from a phosphorus rocket fired to mark the target by a Forward Air Controller (FAC), a pilot in a small prop-driven spotter plane whose duty it was to ensure that bombs fell on the Viet Cong and were not scattered over the countryside. Seldom was the target more substantial than a cluster of grass huts or a few sampans huddled against a river-bank. The weapons used were out of scale with the results; the money spent on a single F-100 sortie could buy dozens of sampans. Secondary explosions, proof that a bomb had found a cache of enemy ammunition, remained relatively few and far between.

But during the Tet offensive, there were plenty of targets to bomb. And nowhere was this more true than at Khe Sanh, a remote outpost in the extreme northwestern corner of South Vietnam. U.S. Marines were based there to monitor the Ho Chi Minh Trail, a few miles to the west. The camp had little apparent importance, yet by late 1967 an estimated 20,000 North Vietnamese troops—two full divisions—had dug into positions surrounding the base. Information pieced together from reconnaissance patrols and a few North Vietnamese defectors indicated the presence of at least 70 heavy artillery pieces, along with 200 or so mortars and a large number of rocket launchers. It appeared that the Communists intended to make Khe Sanh into an American Dienbienphu. The U.S. resolved to hold the camp, no matter what.

The Communist assault began with a cascade of 75-millimeter and 122-millimeter shells; one volley detonated Khe Sanh's main ammunition dump. Then wave upon wave of screaming North Vietnamese stormed the perimeter. The Marines drove them back, and the enemy settled in for a lengthy siege. Each day, from dawn into the night, shells rained down, and in the darkness North Vietnamese patrols could be heard scurrying along the concertina-wire perimeter.

The camp could be reinforced and resupplied only by air; C-130 and

Technicians man a Russian-built SA-2 surface-to-air missile at a launch site in North Vietnam. By 1972, there were 300 such sites scattered around the country; the 35-foot-long two-stage rocket carried a 349-pound high-explosive warhead and could reach altitudes of nearly 60,000 feet.

C-123 transports became Khe Sanh's life line. But the camp owed its ultimate survival to massive air strikes against the enemy positions. On any given day 350 attack fighters of various types—F-4s, A-4s and A-1 Skyraiders, prop-driven planes of World War II vintage—would fly nonstop sorties over the area, their firepower directed by one of several FACs. Often the fighters would be stacked in holding patterns up to 35,000 feet, waiting for a call from a FAC to bomb or strafe a particular gun emplacement or to break up preparations for a ground attack.

The most lethal concentrations of firepower, however, were delivered by a continuing stream of SAC B-52s from Guam, six and a half hours away. Every 90 minutes on average, a "cell" of three bombers would arrive overhead to carpet a rectangle of jungle 1.2 miles long and .6 mile wide with more than 300 bombs. Because of the monsoon overcast, more than half the strikes were guided in by radar—and they were astonishingly accurate. From 25,000 feet, the B-52s could bomb as close as 3,000 feet from the perimeter, or even 1,000 feet in emergencies. Victims rarely heard or saw the planes; the raids were announced by the explosion of the first bomb. Fifteen terrifying seconds later, the attack would be over. Such raids had been flown against the enemy in South Vietnam for two years, but never had they been so devastating. One mission, dropping its bombs less than a mile from Khe Sanh, set off a chain of secondary explosions that lasted two hours.

After two months of this pounding, overlapping craters transformed the battered jungle around Khe Sanh into an eerie moonscape. The battering was more than the two North Vietnamese divisions could take. With losses estimated at 10,000 troops, they melted away, and on April 6, a relief force marched in to mop up the stragglers. The siege of Khe Sanh had been broken.

By then, U.S. and South Vietnamese troops, aided by the withering firepower of the U.S. ground-attack fighters, had long since turned the main thrust of the Tet offensive. The campaign had cost the Viet Cong and North Vietnamese Army the lives of 45,000 men. An additional 7,000 were taken prisoner. American and South Vietnamese losses amounted to less than a tenth of this total. In numbers, the Communists were soundly defeated, and they could ill afford such losses again—but they would not have to. In the U.S., where public support for the conflict had never been more than halfhearted, the Tet offensive was taken as proof that, contrary to government assertions that the War was almost won, the Communists were actually stronger than ever.

The repercussions of these events persuaded President Johnson to declare on March 31, 1968, that he would not seek reelection the following November. Hoping to induce the North Vietnamese and Viet Cong to negotiate, he began to reduce the scope of the air war in the North, first limiting strikes to the area below the 20th Parallel and at the end of October calling a halt to all bombing of the North.

President Richard Nixon, Johnson's successor, then began to send home the half million U.S. troops in South Vietnam, with the intention of turning the War over to the Vietnamese. Several squadrons of jets remained behind, to give air support to the South Vietnamese Army, and air strikes continued covertly against the Ho Chi Minh Trail in Laos and Cambodia. But even this assistance was to end as soon as the South Vietnamese Air Force could be made adequate to the task.

Thus began a period of illusory denouement. For as the Americans systematically withdrew, North Vietnamese troops continued to move down the Ho Chi Minh Trail. By late 1971 they had replenished the losses suffered in the Tet offensive and were again staging commando raids on military posts and airfields in South Vietnam. Truce talks had begun in January 1969, but beyond settling the question of who would sit where at the negotiating table, they had accomplished virtually nothing. Then in the spring of 1972, twelve Communist divisions—comprising 120,000 troops in all—moved south across the 17th Parallel.

At this time, President Nixon was campaigning for reelection with a pledge to end what had become the longest war in American history. He resolved to meet the new offensive with the full force of the nation's aerial might. North Vietnam would be bombed into submission. On April 15, Nixon ordered air strikes to resume. He also lifted many of the restrictions that had shackled U.S. pilots four years earlier. Missions were laid on for more military and industrial targets than had ever been hit before, including some in and around Hanoi and Haiphong: rail yards, bridges, factories, oil depots, airfields, troop-assembly areas. In addition, Navy A-6 Intruders would seed Haiphong harbor with thousands of mines to block the port to Russian and Chinese freighters.

In the four years since American planes had last bombed North Vietnam, airborne weapons of destruction had reached a new level of grim sophistication. The Air Force now had a 2,000-pound bomb with a small television camera in its nose. Named Walleye, it was typically carried by an F-4. Just before bomb release, the back seater adjusted the camera by remote control to center the target in a small TV monitor in front of him, etching the scene in the bomb's electronic memory. After release, the weapon would glide to the target without further attention from the GIB. Another variety of so-called smart bomb depended on a laser beam for its extraordinary accuracy. This weapon required at least two planes, one to shine the beam on the target and another to drop the bomb. Usually the bomb struck within a few feet of the spot illuminated by the laser, and since bombs from two or more aircraft could home in on the same beam, the result was a concentration of explosive power unimaginable with conventional bombs.

Yet the task of dropping any bomb on North Vietnam had become manifestly more dangerous. During the bombing halt, the North Vietnamese had greatly improved their antiaircraft defenses. Now there were nearly 300 SAM sites, many equipped with a new, more accurate version of the SA-2. The number of radar-directed flak batteries had increased to more than 1,500. And an estimated 250 interceptors—

Outlined against the glare of arc lights, an Air Force F-4 Phantom crew goes over a preflight check list as ground personnel ready the jet for an early-morning takeoff from South Vietnam's Phan Rang airfield. Unlike Navy Phantoms, Air Force F-4s had a complete set of flying controls for the weapons systems operator in the rear seat.

one third of them the fast, agile MiG-21s—had arrived in the North.

The first mission of this new campaign, dubbed Operation *Linebacker* by football fan Nixon, was launched on May 10, 1972. A force of 32 F-4s from the 8th Tactical Fighter Wing lifted off from Ubon Air Base and headed north toward Thud Ridge. Their target: the Paul Doumer Bridge, repaired and, like the Dragon's Jaw, strong as ever. Suspended from the wings and bellies of the planes was a calculated mix of TV- and laser-guided weapons and 500-pound conventional bombs.

An armada of supporting craft moved with them. Typically, F-105 Wild Weasels from the 388th TFW flew in first with an escort of Phantoms to attack antiaircraft defenses and look out for MiGs. Then came another flight of F-4s assigned to strew the skies with chaff— aluminum foil cut into strips, intended to confound the enemy's radar. Fifteen minutes later—the chaff needed time to spread—the main strike force would roll in over the target. To either side, additional F-4s would fly close escort and MiGCAP, each plane armed with Sparrow and Sidewinder missiles.

The most coveted assignment of the day was given to eight F-4s from the 555th Tactical Fighter Squadron—the Triple Nickel. The planes flew lead MiGCAP, ranging farther afield to intercept MiGs before they could attack. Besides all these combat aircraft, there was the usual complement of tankers, reconnaissance planes and air-rescue craft, plus four EB-66s to disrupt enemy radar. Altogether, nearly 130 planes took part, though less than half the force actually dropped bombs.

The lead Phantoms streamed toward the Paul Doumer Bridge, and soon flight after flight was dropping its bombs. Despite the havoc wrought among the defenders by Wild Weasels, the flak remained heavy and the polelike SAMs continued to vault upward—160 of them before the day was over. Even so, the blitz of chaff and the EB-66s' jamming efforts had apparently done their work; the Phantoms moved off target with the loss of only a single escort.

While the strike force was pummeling the bridge, the F-4s flying MiGCAP had taken up a blocking position to the north. Oyster Flight, under Major Robert Lodge, soon noted four blips on its radarscopes, at a distance of about 45 miles. The two forces closed on each other at more than 1,000 miles an hour; they had about three minutes before meeting. Lodge was well north of all other American aircraft in the vicinity, so he knew the dots on his radar had to be the enemy—MiG-21s from Yen Bai airfield near Hanoi, as it happened. The MiGs had not yet come into view when Lodge's back seater, Captain Roger Locher, locked the Phantom's fire-control radar onto the lead plane. Seconds later, at a range of eight miles, Lodge squeezed off a Sparrow.

The missile leaped from the launcher, then exploded. The mechanism inside the missile that arms the warhead after launch had malfunctioned, detonating the Sparrow prematurely. Lodge immediately fired his second missile. By now he was only six miles from his target. Five long seconds ticked by as the missile searched out its quarry at three times the speed of sound. Then it hit, and 60 pounds of explosives in the warhead turned the MiG into a gout of orange flame.

Meanwhile, Lodge's wingman, First Lieutenant John Markle, had locked onto the second MiG and had squeezed off two Sparrows in rapid succession. The first would have sufficed; it struck just behind the canopy, setting the enemy plane afire and cutting it in two.

The third and fourth MiGs, in a desperate ploy to drive off the Phantoms, pumped out a fusillade of Atoll missiles. Only luck could have brought a hit, for the Atolls were approaching head on and thus could not home in on the hot gases blasting from the F-4's tailpipes. Captain Richard S. Ritchie, leader of Oyster Flight's second element, roared after the two enemy planes as they shot past. "There were missiles in the air all over the place," he recalled, "fireballs, smoke trails, debris and airplanes everywhere." Undaunted, he pulled his Phantom into a climbing right turn that put him directly behind the trailing MiG. His back seater, Captain Charles Debellevue, locked his radar onto the enemy plane, and Ritchie fired two Sparrows. The first passed wide of the mark, but the second one connected. For the third time in about 30 seconds, a MiG-21 was converted into an intense orange fireball.

That left one MiG still flying, and Lodge bore in after it. Abruptly,

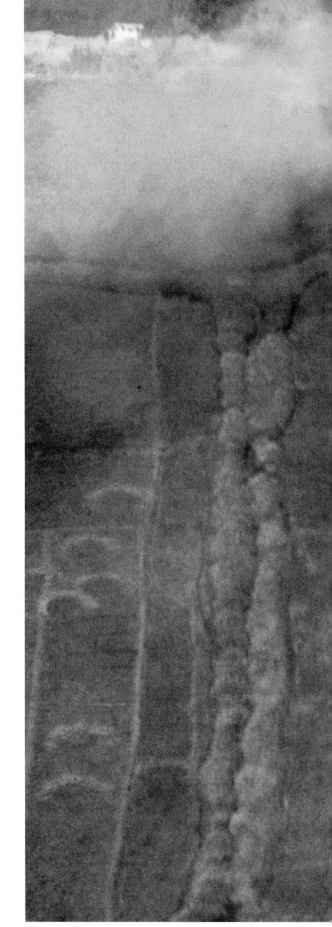

Streaming vapor trails after a 500-mph dive, an Air Force F-4 Phantom fires a rocket salvo at guerrillas entrenched in a South Vietnamese hamlet.

he was in trouble. Four MiG-19s screamed down out of nowhere.

"Oyster Lead, you have MiGs at your 10 o'clock," his wingman called. But Lodge, intent on pursuit, made no response.

"Hey, Lead, break right, break right! They are firing at you!"

But it was too late. The F-4 heaved and crumpled, then exploded. Lodge perished, but Locher somehow managed to eject. He landed in a forest near Thud Ridge and evaded capture for 23 days before a rescue helicopter lifted him out. The rest of Oyster Flight lit afterburners and sped home, easily outrunning the slower MiG-19s. Ritchie and Debellevue reported their victory—the first of five that would make them aces and the top Air Force MiG killers in Vietnam. Later, Debellevue, flying in the back seat with a different pilot, would get credit for yet another MiG. His total of six was the highest score for an American in this war.

Ritchie and crew would not be the first, however, to win ace's laurels in Vietnam. That distinction went to a pair of Navy lieutenants, Randy Cunningham and his GIB, William Driscoll. On the opening day of *Linebacker,* carrier pilots were sent to attack the rail yards in Haiphong. Cunningham and Driscoll already had two kills in their Phantom, and before the day was out, they would shoot down three MiG-17s.

The action began as Cunningham pulled up from his bombing run. Two MiG-17s slipped in behind him, and one started firing. Cunningham's wingman could not help. Though he was behind the MiGs, he was afraid of hitting Cunningham if he fired his missiles, and his F-4 had no gun. Cunningham turned sharply toward his attacker, who because he was traveling so fast, could not follow the maneuver and shot ahead of him. Reversing his turn to get behind the MiG, Cunningham launched a Sidewinder that streaked out and nailed the enemy plane.

Looking around for more MiGs to fight, Cunningham spotted eight of them swarming around three fellow F-4s. As he dived to help, one of the Navy jets streaked past with three MiGs chasing it. Cunningham intended to take on the lead MiG, but so close had it come to the Phantom that he could not fire his Sidewinder for fear of hitting the wrong plane. He had no choice but to fall in behind the MiG and radio the Phantom pilot to break sharply away—thus giving him a clear shot. During these few seconds, four MiG-17s had attached themselves to Cunningham's tail. As Driscoll, in the back, gave warning each time the lead MiG trained its guns on them, Cunningham changed course slightly to throw off the pilot's aim. At last, the Phantom heading this parade reversed its turn, and Cunningham fired a Sidewinder. The MiG ahead of him burst into flame. He then deftly slipped away from the MiG-17 behind him— and from four MiG-21s that had joined the fray. Approximately two minutes had elapsed since Cunningham had dropped his bombs.

"Everywhere I looked there were MiGs," he said later, "and I didn't see any other F-4s around. So I headed east," back toward his carrier, the *Constellation.* Just as he reached the coast, he spotted a lone MiG-17 approaching head on. Cunningham and Driscoll were alone, too, their wingman having drifted off during the earlier melee. But Cunning-

In the radar room of Saigon's Tan Son Nhut Airport, air controllers direct warplanes to a target area near the Cambodian border, plotting their courses on a huge transparent map. As the planes neared their objective, an airborne forward controller pinpointed the target area for them.

123

ham was as aggressive as any pilot in Vietnam, and eager for a fifth kill. He jammed his throttle full ahead. "Watch this, Willie," he said to Driscoll, expecting that the MiG would take evasive action. But the pilot held course—and started firing his 23-millimeter and 37-millimeter cannon. "His whole nose lit up like a Christmas tree!" recalled Cunningham, who zoomed to dodge the shells.

Most MiG-17s would have swept by and headed home. But this one stayed to fight and in seconds had maneuvered alongside the Navy jet. I looked over, said Cunningham, "and there was the MiG, canopy to canopy with me. He couldn't have been more than 30 feet away. I could see the pilot clearly—leather helmet, goggles, scarf."

The Phantom was ill suited to a classic one-on-one dogfight with the MiG-17; in most such contests, jets fly at subsonic speeds, where the MiG is more agile than an F-4. But a dogfight is what now occurred. Both planes were climbing nearly straight up and losing speed, the MiG dropping behind and putting Cunningham squarely in his sights. The pilot started shooting. Cunningham rolled out of the line of fire, then dived to escape. For a second or two Cunningham flew away from the MiG, then turned back to reengage. By that time the MiG was coming at him again. The Phantom snapped up and rolled, repeating the first maneuver. The MiG recovered and came at him. And so it went: "Up into a rolling scissors—advantage—disadvantage—disengaged—came back—and up into the vertical again." Neither plane could find the narrow edge that would bring victory.

Then at the top of a climb and probably low on fuel, the MiG broke off the engagement and fled—nearly straight down. Cunningham dived after the MiG, loosed a Sidewinder and watched it connect. There was a quick flash, a puff of smoke, and the jet flew into the ground.

Never had Cunningham and Driscoll fought so perilous a duel. And no wonder. Later intelligence reports suggested that the downed pilot was none other than Colonel Toon, the enemy's leading ace. Before his demise, Colonel Toon, by Communist count, had shot down 13 American planes, the highest score, if true, of any pilot in the War.

But the day was not yet over for Cunningham and Driscoll. Their battle with Toon had attracted other MiGs, and the two new aces just barely escaped with the help of another Phantom, which happened along at the right moment. Then two SAMs came hurtling toward them. Cunningham saw the first in time to dodge it, but the second came upon him so quickly he could not take evasive action; it exploded about 400 feet away. Shrapnel from the blast damaged the aircraft's hydraulic system. A minute later, as the hydraulic fluid leaked away, Cunningham was fighting with every nerve and muscle to control the aircraft—and to get as far as the Gulf of Tonkin so that he and Driscoll would not have to bail out into North Vietnamese hands.

Just as they crossed the coastline, the controls failed completely, and the Phantom began to spin. With a crash now inevitable, the two men ejected. U.S. ships, which had been monitoring the seaward progress of the jet, had dispatched helicopters to pick up survivors. In minutes, the two fliers were winched from the sea and carried to safety.

All in all it had been a good day for the Phantoms. The Haiphong rail yard had been pulverized by the Navy's F-4s. The Air Force had succeeded in destroying a span of the Paul Doumer Bridge, closing it to traffic. Three days later the Phantoms streaked north to smother the Dragon's Jaw in 40 tons of laser- and television-guided explosives. It went down—for the first time, and the last.

In six months, Operation *Linebacker* had utterly ravaged North Vietnam's transportation system and other targets as well. Yet the Communists continued to stall the peace talks in Paris and on December 13 walked out of them. The U.S. response was to prepare more attacks. On December 18, *Linebacker II* began. SAC B-52s would conduct a virtually nonstop bombardment of Hanoi and Haiphong, a maximum effort so intense that when it was over it would be called the Eleven-Day War. Their targets—industries, airfields and transportation facilities that had as yet been spared—lay in the heart of Hanoi and Haiphong.

Until now, bombing missions had been safe ones for SAC crews; the B-52s could fly well above the highest-shooting flak in South Vietnam or Cambodia. There were no SAMs or MiGs in these areas. Over Hanoi, however, the bombers braved 100-millimeter flak and thickets of SAMs. "Hold your hand at arm's length, fingers bunched and pointed toward your eyes," said one pilot. "Now move your hand toward your face, fast, and spread your fingers. Those damned SAMs looked like that going by." The cost was high: 15 bombers lost for 729 sorties flown.

But by the time the strikes were over, the B-52s had pulverized their objectives with 15,000 tons of bombs. Nothing of value to the war effort in Hanoi and Haiphong escaped ruin. More than 1,600 military structures had been hit, and 10 airfields had been knocked out of operation. Approximately three million gallons of oil and fuel had been torched, and the strands of North Vietnam's rail net had been severed in more than 500 places. On January 1, 1973, as a result of this onslaught, North Vietnam agreed to resume the peace talks. Twenty-two days later, a cease-fire was signed. For American jets and their pilots, the war against North Vietnam was over.

The cost had been extravagantly high, in both dollars and lives. More than 6.3 million tons of bombs were dropped in Indochina between 1964 and 1973—a figure that eclipses the total used against both Germany and Japan in World War II by a factor of three. The jets of the Vietnam era cost up to nine million dollars apiece, and the U.S. lost 2,400 of them in Southeast Asia—more than 1,800 to enemy action— at a cost of something like 2,000 pilots and crewmen.

Two years after the Americans had gone home, the very catastrophe occurred that they had tried to prevent. In late March of 1975, a rejuvenated North Vietnamese Army began what would be its final offensive. South Vietnamese resistance crumbled, and four tumultuous weeks later, Saigon fell. The Communist North had won the War. ◆◆

A crewman on the Constellation waits by a catapult-control station during the launch of an F-8 Crusader in the Gulf of Tonkin in 1972.

Thunder from the sea

When, in March of 1965, the U.S. initiated the massive bombing campaign against North Vietnam known as *Rolling Thunder,* the Navy was on hand to make a major contribution. Operating from carriers off the enemy coast, Navy fighter-bombers pounded targets in North Vietnam and flew thousands of sorties in support of ground forces.

Vietnam became the acid test for a generation of Navy jets that had entered service since Korea. The LTV F-8 Crusader *(left),* a 34,000-pound fighter armed with cannon and missiles, was as heavy as many World War II medium bombers. The Navy also fielded a trio of rugged strike aircraft: the Douglas A-4 Skyhawk, the Vought A-7 Corsair II and the all-weather Grumman A-6 Intruder.

To handle these formidable jets, angled flight decks replaced straight platforms, permitting simultaneous launchings and recoveries with greater safety. Powerful steam catapults could shove heavily loaded planes aloft far more efficiently than earlier hydraulic ones. And returning pilots were guided in by precise mirror landing systems (MLS) instead of by signal officers waving colored paddles.

An ordnanceman wheels a pair of Sidewinder air-to-air missiles past a row of A-6 all-weather attack planes aboard the carrier Constellation. Most of the 59 MiGs destroyed in air-to-air combat by Navy pilots during the Vietnam War were shot down with this weapon.

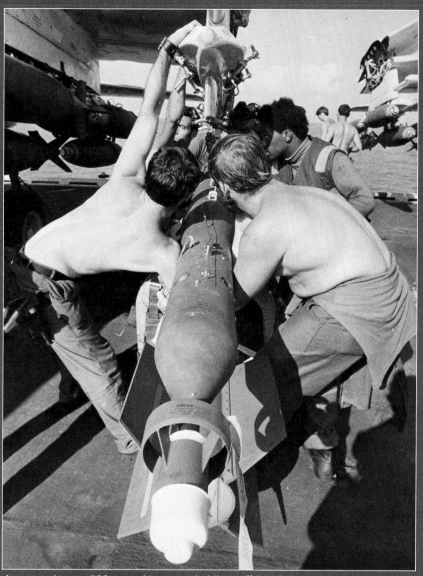

Armorers hoist a 500-pound laser-guided "smart" bomb into position.

Conventional high-explosive "iron" bombs bristle from the weapons racks of planes being armed for a mission. Fuses that fit into the holes on the bombs' noses were screwed on just before takeoff in order to minimize the danger of explosions.

Catapult crewmen on the Hancock attach
the catapult bridle to an A-4 Skyhawk as the
plane director raises his arms, signaling
the pilot to release the aircraft's brakes.

A plane captain sprints alongside his aircraft
as it taxis prior to launch, while a crewman
pulls the landing-gear safety pins. The men
wore headphones for communication and
for protection from the shriek of the engines.

Steam generated by the catapult launch of an A-7 Corsair II swirls over the Enterprise's flight deck. The catapult could accelerate an airplane from a standstill to more than 170 mph in less than three seconds.

An F-8, its image blurred by the impact of landing, streaks across the flight deck before its tail hook catches the arrester cable and brings the plane to a stop. The crewman running toward it was ready to release the jet from the cable if its tail hook did not disengage automatically.

An emergency nylon barricade on the Oriskany snares an A-4 flown by a wounded pilot. Although his legs were broken, he completed his bomb run before returning to the aircraft carrier 125 miles away.

5

Duels over the desert

All through the spring of 1967, the high-pitched voice of Egypt's President Gamal Abdel Nasser lashed out over Cairo radio, churning up old hatreds. "We are confronting Israel," he cried in May, "and the West as well—the West which created Israel, which despises us, the Arabs. . . ." His words sent a stab of anxiety through a world already on edge over the war in Vietnam, and over the continued hostility between the United States and Russia. The West was in fact supporting Israel with money and arms; and large quantities of guns, tanks and airplanes were arriving in Egypt from the Soviet Union. War would be total, Nasser boasted, "and our objective will be to destroy Israel."

Tension in the Middle East had been bowstring taut for nearly 20 years, and twice already the arrows had been loosed. In May 1948, two days after Israel was established as an independent state in the ancient land of Palestine, its Arab neighbors, adamantly opposed to the new Jewish nation, launched an invasion to crush it. Egypt, Jordan, Lebanon, Syria and Iraq all sent in troops—though with little success. Eight months later, when the United Nations arranged a truce, Israel had increased its territory by nearly half. Resentment simmered—the Arabs determined to reclaim Palestine, the Israelis holding on for very survival.

Then in 1956, fighting broke out anew. Nasser, in a bold political stroke, nationalized the Suez Canal, which was owned by the British government and private French investors. When Britain and France attempted to reclaim it, Israel jumped in to help, but to no avail. The war lasted less than three months and the U.N. again restored the peace; Nasser kept the canal.

Less than 10 years later, tensions were again approaching the boiling point. Large numbers of Arab refugees, fleeing Palestine during Israel's War of Independence, had tented down in the desert along Israel's borders. From here they launched commando raids into Israel. At first these forays had been sporadic and disorganized, but in 1964 the guerrillas had banded together in a loose confederation called the Palestine Liberation Organization (PLO), dedicated to Israel's overthrow.

In November 1966, the Israelis retaliated against Jordan for allowing the PLO to operate from its soil. Using tanks, they attacked a refugee center in Samu, demolishing 127 buildings, among them a school and a medical clinic. Five months later, Israel struck again—in Syria, where artillery on the Golan Heights had been lobbing shells at nearby Israeli

Flying a U.S.-made Skyhawk, an Israeli pilot fires a deadly salvo of rockets at Syrian positions during the 1973 Yom Kippur War. "Knowing your request for air support will be answered by Skyhawks," said one Israeli, "does wonders for your morale."

farm workers. On April 7, 1967, a squadron of French-built Dassault Mirages, Israel's newest supersonic jets, screamed in to knock out the guns. The Syrians scrambled a force of MiG-21s, and in the ensuing dogfight the Israelis downed six of the Soviet-supplied fighters.

Smarting from this defeat, the Syrians turned for help to Nasser, with whom they had signed a mutual defense pact. Nasser had built Egypt into the most powerful nation on Israel's borders. Its ground forces numbered 500,000 men, with nearly 2,000 tanks supplied by Russia. Egypt boasted an Air Force of nearly 600 Russian-built planes, among them four squadrons of MiG-19s, six of MiG-21s and one of Sukhoi Su-7 fighter-bombers; there were also two squadrons of Tupolev Tu-16s, twin-jet bombers capable of reaching any Israeli city within 15 minutes.

For months the Egyptian President had been berating Israel over Cairo radio. Now he backed his bluster with steel. On May 15, Egyptian infantry, tanks and artillery began moving across the Suez bridges and into the Sinai desert on Israel's southwestern border; the next day they ousted U.N. peace-keeping troops. On the 20th, Nasser sent an air-borne battalion to Sharm el-Sheikh, near the mouth of the Gulf of Aqaba. Two days later he closed the gulf to ships bound for Israel's port at Elath. By then, Egypt had 100,000 troops in the Sinai, along with

Stopped in their tracks by strafing Israeli jets on the third day of the Six-Day War, Egyptian military vehicles lie wrecked on the approaches to Mitla Pass, a strategic objective in the western Sinai.

1,000 tanks. Events seemed to be heading rapidly toward a major crisis.

Israel had lived too long with the specter of its own annihilation to be caught unprepared. Its small Army was well equipped and superbly trained, and the Air Force had built up a formidable arsenal of jets supplied by France. In 1955 it had purchased 75 Dassault Ouragon fighter-bombers, comparable to the F-84 Thunderjet. To these it soon added Dassault's sweptwing Mystère IV, a near equivalent of the F-86 Sabre. Then came squadrons of Sud-Aviation Vautour light bombers, Fouga Magister ground-attack planes—a French design built in Israel—and, in 1959, the fast, nimble Super-Mystère B2, Western Europe's first supersonic interceptor.

The Super-Mystères were a match for the top-line Arab fighter of the 1950s, the MiG-19. But by 1962 the Russians had begun arming their clients with the more formidable MiG-21. Only one European aircraft could match it: Dassault's delta-winged Mirage III. A superb dogfighter, with a top speed of 1,460 miles per hour, the Mirage III could outpace and outshoot any plane in the Arab arsenal with its two 30-millimeter cannon and two American-supplied Sidewinder missiles. It could also haul two 1,000-pound bombs, and its 750-mile combat range could carry it to targets deep within Arab territory. Israel ordered 40 of them.

Flying low through gaps in Egyptian radar defenses, Israeli jets destroyed these MiG-21s, seen on the tarmac of an unidentified base. On the first day of the War, the Israelis knocked out more than 300 Arab aircraft.

By the tense spring of 1967, Israel's Air Force could deploy nearly 300 aircraft, including transports and support planes; the Arabs had close to 850. Only skill in combat could make up the difference. Said Brigadier General Ezer Weizmann, chief of air operations, "We always went on the assumption that we would be fighting the finest air force in the world—then we set out to show that this was not the case."

Every day, the likelihood of war seemed to increase. Israeli reconnaissance flights revealed the awesome extent of the Arab build-up. By May 26, infantry from Egypt and Iraq had moved into Jordan and, with Jordanian forces, was massing along Israel's eastern border. Arab artillery could easily hit Israeli population centers like Tel Aviv, just 12 miles to the west on the Mediterranean coast.

For weeks Israel's diplomats had been trying to defuse the situation, but the country had also prepared for battle. On May 20, the government began to mobilize Israel's 200,000-man reserve. On June 1, a

A pair of Algerian MiG-17s—sent to reinforce the hard-hit Egyptian Air Force during the Six-Day War—attacks the vanguard of an Israeli column sweeping through the northern Sinai toward the Suez Canal. The Arab air strike failed to slow the column, and the Israelis captured the canal on the 7th of June, 1967.

hurried shuffle of Cabinet officers brought Moshe Dayan, Israel's most venerated warrior, to the post of Minister of Defense. Still, Israel appeared to be courting peace. At a press conference the next day Dayan declared: ''The government, before I became a member of it, was embarked on diplomacy: We must give it a chance.'' And that Saturday, June 3, large numbers of Israeli soldiers on weekend passes could be seen splashing about at the Mediterranean beaches.

It was a masterly deception. Monday, June 5, at 7:45 a.m., the Israelis attacked. Light bombers and attack planes—Vautours, Ouragons, Mystères, Magisters, Super-Mystères and Mirage IIIs—screamed down on the major air bases in northern Egypt and the Sinai. These opening strikes hit 10 airfields. The jets, in flights of four, made three or four passes over each target—bombing and strafing hangars, control towers, runways and parked airplanes of every description. Thirty-two MiG-21s were destroyed at various fields as they taxied for takeoff. Only eight others managed to get airborne during the first strike; they accounted for just two Israeli planes before being shot down themselves.

Israel's gambit was a daring one; the Air Force had held back only 12 fighters to defend against counterattack. But Egypt had been caught by surprise. Opening air strikes generally occur at dawn; with this hazardous hour past, the Egyptians had let down their guard. Early-morning fighter patrols had already returned to base. There had been no telltale blips on Egyptian radar screens; the attackers had flown as low as 30 feet above the desert. No radio chatter had given them away.

Among the leaders of the first strike was Major Aharon "Yalo" Shavit, a stocky, blue-eyed veteran of the 1956 Suez fighting with Egypt. Precisely on schedule, Yalo's flight of four Super-Mystères swept down on the MiG-21 base at Inchas, near Cairo. On the first run Yalo gouged deep craters in the runway with a pair of conventional 500-pound bombs. Behind him, other squadron members unleashed an Israeli weapon called the Dibber, designed expressly for wrecking runways. A small rocket in its tail drove it through the steel-reinforced concrete of the airstrip. There it would lie until exploded seconds or minutes later by a time fuse, terrorizing ground crews assigned to repair duty.

His bombs released, Yalo made three strafing passes over the field, and on each one he ripped open a parked MiG. Then he was in trouble. On his last pass he caught a spray of bullets from a Russian-built 14.7-millimeter heavy machine gun. Four rounds smashed into the cockpit close to his seat, and others activated his speed brake, locking it open. When he arrived back at his air base, his landing gear would not extend.

''Bail out!'' came the order from the ground.

''What do you mean, bail out!'' Yalo shot back. Why waste a frontline fighter that just might fly again?

Pulling up the jet's nose just short of a stall—thereby cutting his speed—Yalo aimed for the far end of the landing strip; should he crash, the wreckage would not close the field to planes coming in behind him. There was a jolt and a plume of sparks as the crippled jet skidded along

139

the pavement and into the dirt beyond. Then quiet. Yalo climbed down from the cockpit and strolled to the debriefing room to report on his mission—and to pick up his orders for the next one.

For nearly three hours the air strikes continued, rolling in at 10-minute intervals, and the Egyptians could do little to stop them. Antiaircraft gunners scored a few hits before their weapons were silenced, but not enough to matter. Russian SA-2 missiles, acquired by Egypt along with MiGs and other Soviet military gear, proved virtually useless. With an effective minimum altitude of 2,000 feet, they failed to connect with a single low-flying Israeli jet.

The few MiGs that managed to take off were quickly overwhelmed. When 20 MiG-19s and MiG-21s reached the battle zone from Hurghada in the south, they were already short of fuel. All either were shot down by Israeli jets or crash-landed when they ran out of fuel.

By midmorning, as the last Israeli jet moved off its target, the most powerful Air Force in the Middle East had been all but erased. More than a score of airfields had been blasted by the end of the War's first day. Only one runway—in the northern Sinai—escaped incapacitating damage; the Israelis were saving it for themselves, to fly supplies in and evacuate casualties. Of Egypt's 340 combat aircraft, 300 would never fly again. Most had been demolished on the ground by cannon fire, including all 30 of Egypt's Tu-16s, the planes capable of bombing Israel.

With the Egyptian Air Force out of the battle, the Israelis turned their sights on targets to the east—airfields in Syria, Jordan and Iraq. That same day, Yalo led his Super-Mystères to Amman, Jordan, where he blasted the runway and knocked out three neatly parked British-built Hawker Hunter attack jets. Then just after 4 p.m., he took off again, bound for a Syrian air base at Zaikal, northeast of Damascus. Nearing the city, he encountered an Israeli flight returning from an earlier strike. A warning crackled over his radio: "There are MiGs covering the area."

Yalo had already met the MiG in mock combat. The previous year a disgruntled Iraqi pilot had fled to Israel with a late-model MiG-21, and Israel's Air Force had put it through its paces. At all but the lowest altitudes, the Russian plane won handily against all comers except the Mirage; but near the deck its performance suffered. "We knew exactly what to do," recalled Yalo, "come in low, at 100 feet." But to make his dive onto a target he first had to gain altitude. Checking the sky and seeing no threat, he led his flight to 6,000 feet. Then he nosed down for a low-level pass over the Zaikal runways.

So fast is the closing rate of supersonic jets that even the most experienced pilot may find himself caught unawares. As Yalo released his bombs and banked left, he counted the planes lined up behind him. There were five: his own three flight members—and a pair of MiG-21s. He had been bounced from nowhere. "Number Four, break right, break right," he called to the tail-end Charlie of his formation.

Number Four swerved sharply, the lead MiG close behind. Yalo wrenched his Mystère around toward the MiG's tail. At the same in-

The all-seeing eye

Among the strangest-looking aircraft in the skies today is a modified Boeing 707 jet with a great revolving disk on its back. Yet for all its ungainliness, it is one of the crucial planes in the U.S. arsenal—nothing less than a skyborne radar station with a 360-degree field of view reaching to the horizon. Called AWACS, for Airborne Warning and Control System, it offers the U.S. and its allies a measure of security against surprise attack by the planes of a hostile nation.

Its radar antennas, housed in the disk, scan the airspace from the earth's surface to the stratosphere. Before the advent of AWACS—which can remain aloft for 21 hours with in-flight refueling—airborne aggressors might have escaped detection by flying close to the ground. (Earthbound radar cannot track low-altitude aircraft, while most airborne systems cannot distinguish a low-flying plane from a tree or building.) AWACS radar, however, readily picks up ground-hugging aircraft by emitting a special signal that returns at a different frequency when reflected from a moving object.

Processing these radar returns, an onboard computer calculates the elevation, velocity, range and heading of every aircraft in the AWACS' 120,000-square-mile purview. In a war, friendly craft would identify themselves by a code. Data on the remaining planes would then be relayed to strategists on land or at sea, and used to vector allied fighters to enemy aircraft. Just how AWACS works is shown on the following pages.

Measuring 30 feet in diameter and six feet in depth, AWACS' revolving disk (top right) feeds data to radar technicians (right) aboard the jet. Seated here before three of the plane's nine consoles, technicians chart the course of all aircraft over a selected area.

Skyborne link to ground and sea

This diagram illustrates the multiplicity of functions a single AWACS can perform in war. After detecting enemy aircraft at sea *(black planes, below)*, the AWACS contacts an aircraft carrier either by radio directly or via satellite. This prompts the dispatch of carrier-based interceptors *(white planes)*, which are then guided to their targets by technicians aboard the AWACS or on the carrier.

At the same time, AWACS is in touch with several land-based stations—a battlefield headquarters that relays instructions to tanks, an antiaircraft-missile battery and an inland airfield from which rocket-equipped interceptors rise to engage intruders, seen approaching from the other side of the mountains. Unlike the ground-based radar, AWACS can "see" the enemy planes, and once more it is able to transmit instructions for guiding both missiles and planes to targets.

stant, Yalo's wingman turned in smart pursuit of the second MiG.

Both Syrian pilots were well aware of the MiG's limitations at low altitude. They zoomed out of range of the slower-climbing Israeli jets. Now Yalo had to bring his opponent back down again. "So I gave him my belly," he recalled. "When he saw that I had turned on my back and couldn't follow, he decided to come down and get me."

That was the Syrian's mistake. As the MiG shrieked toward him, Yalo rolled upright and tucked in behind the enemy's tail. A quick blast of 30-millimeter cannon fire sent the Syrian crashing into the sand dunes. Then Yalo glanced toward his wingman, who was rounding up behind the second MiG.

Young and unseasoned, the wingman was not certain what to do next. "Number One, this is Number Two," he radioed.

"For Christ's sake, what do you want?" Yalo replied.

"I've got the MiG in my . . ."

"PRESS THE TRIGGER!"

Number Two complied. "Oops, the wing separated from his aircraft," he reported. Then the Mystères turned for home.

Israel's Air Force had been flying for nearly 10 hours straight. Each plane was being exploited to capacity. By performing only the absolute essentials of refueling and rearming, the Israelis had cut the turn-around time between sorties to less than half an hour, and in some crack squadrons to an astonishing seven and a half minutes. A pilot might report back from a strike, grab a cup of coffee or a bite of sandwich, and be back in the air again before he could finish his snack. At that pace, a few flew as many as nine missions on the War's first day.

The next morning the Israeli pilots took to the air again. Some ran follow-up strikes against Arab airfields, radar installations and gun positions. Others flew in support of Israeli tank battalions as they pushed the Egyptian Army out of the Sinai and across the Suez Canal, or blasted Syrian troops that were dug into the escarpments of the Golan Heights. Occasionally, a Mirage or Mystère would meet up with a lone Arab MiG, and often as not would score a kill. But by the end of the second day the air war was over. The Israelis had put out of commission all but one Arab airfield within 375 miles, demolished 393 aircraft on the ground and 23 in the air. They had lost only 26 planes, most of them to antiaircraft fire.

It was among the most one-sided victories in half a century of air warfare. And now, with the skies cleared of Arab fighters, the Israeli Army could roll across the desert with relative ease. By the time a cease-fire was called, on June 10, they had seized the entire Sinai Peninsula, the Golan Heights, the narrow Gaza Strip along the Mediterranean coast, the West Bank of the Jordan River and the Arab section of divided Jerusalem. In just six days, the Jewish state had neutralized its enemies and nearly doubled the land under its control.

Israel's victory established a comfortable buffer of occupied territory, but it brought no lasting security; the Arabs wanted their land back. Within months, the Russians resupplied Egypt and Syria with MiGs and guns, tanks and missiles. During the next two years the rhetoric of violence issued forth unabated from Arab capitals, and Palestinian guerrillas continued their raids from Jordan. The Israelis, in turn, began building a chain of bunkers and concrete gun emplacements in the western Sinai along the Suez Canal. To the Egyptians these fortifications—called the Bar Lev Line, after a prominent Israeli general—symbolized a status quo they could not accept. In September 1968, Egypt began shelling the Israeli positions from the canal's west bank.

So began the War of Attrition, a dreary period of border skirmishes intended to grind down Israel's Army. Without the resources for an extended artillery duel, the Israelis sat out the Egyptian barrages in the cover of their bunkers. As long as casualties stayed low, Israel made no serious effort to silence the guns.

But the Egyptians escalated the conflict. In early March 1969, they hurled more than 35,000 artillery shells across the canal in just two days, killing many Israeli troops. For relief, Israel called on its Air Force.

By now Israel had started buying planes from the U.S. The sturdy McDonnell Douglas A-4 Skyhawk fighter-bomber was already in service, and F-4 Phantoms were to arrive in September. Few of these new planes were equipped with electronic-countermeasure (ECM) devices intended to help a pilot evade radar-directed SAMs and flak. But during the next few years, Israel would install the black boxes in many of its jets.

On a typical cross-canal mission, a force of Skyhawks under a top cover of Mirages would hit antiaircraft batteries, SA-2 missile sites and radar installations. Then a follow-up strike would assail the artillery. As the months wore on, guerrillas operating from Jordan and Syria joined in the battle. Soon after the heavy Egyptian artillery barrages, Israel was staging air attacks all along the fringes of the lands it had occupied.

It was dogged, dangerous work. "We bombed the borders almost every day," one pilot recalled. "Training missions in the mornings, and bombing runs in the afternoon." Sometimes the attackers would be intercepted by MiGs, but the main hazard was the lethal network of ground defenses. The Israelis could easily avoid the SA-2s by flying low, but now they came up against the radar-directed ZSU-23, a battery of four 23-millimeter cannon that fired 4,000 rounds a minute. "You fly into a rain of bullets," one flight leader said.

Several aircraft were shot down, and even though dozens of Egyptian guns were knocked out in return, the Arab shelling continued. More drastic measures were needed. So in January 1970, Israel's new Phantoms began striking deep into Egypt's Nile Delta to pound radar and missile sites in the vicinity of Cairo itself. Most of Egypt's missile and antiaircraft positions were manned by Soviet personnel. The Russians, alarmed by the havoc the Phantoms were causing, sent five squadrons of the latest-model MiG-21s, along with 150 Soviet pilots to fly them.

A confrontation soon occurred. On July 30, a formation of 16 MiGs jumped a flight of Phantoms over the Gulf of Suez, and were in turn bounced by Israeli Mirages flying overhead. In the ensuing free-for-all,

Two F-15 Eagles climb virtually straight up, then level off upside down. The maneuver, completed by rolling the plane right side up, allows a pilot to go from vertical to horizontal without suffering the discomfort of blood rushing to his head—a phenomenon known as redout—that would result if he leveled off by pushing the plane's nose down at the apex of his climb.

the Israelis proved to be more than a match for their Soviet opponents.

"I succeeded in getting my sights on a MiG," said one Phantom pilot, and his back seater established a radar lock on the target. "At a range of 1,000 meters," said the pilot, "we fired a missile. The MiG exploded into a flaming ball but, surprisingly, flew on. We fired another missile, but this was no longer necessary. The Russian plane suddenly disintegrated in the air." Somehow, its pilot managed to eject. Four other Russians—but no Israelis—were shot down during the fight.

Neither Russia nor the U.S. wanted to risk war over the Middle East, and so both powers started pressuring their clients to desist. Israel and Egypt, seeing little profit in continuing as they were, signed a cease-fire on August 7, 1970. Once again the violence subsided.

The following month, Nasser fell dead of a heart attack, and his successor, Anwar al-Sadat, set out to win through diplomacy what his country had lost in battle. He had little chance of success. Israel, ensconced behind borders that seemed, at last, strategically sound, saw no reason to give them up unless forced to do so. And that was unlikely. "Israel is now a military superpower," blustered Major General Ariel Sharon, the most hawkish official in Jerusalem. "Every national force in Europe is weaker than we are. We can conquer in one week the area from Khartoum to Baghdad and Algeria." Faced with such intransigence, Sadat and his Arab allies began gearing for another war.

Russian-built planes poured into Egypt and Syria. Over the next three years, Syria built up its Air Force to number 360 fighters and bombers. During the same period, the Egyptian Air Force grew to 650 aircraft, including MiG-21s and MiG-17s armed with missiles, MiG-19s, Su-7s and a squadron of Tu-16 strategic bombers. Egypt's pilots started training with inspired dedication. Sadat had learned from 1967. When war came, he would make the first devastating strike.

On the ground, the Arabs had dramatically improved their antiaircraft defenses. To a refurbished network of SA-2 installations along the canal, the Egyptians had added between 75 and 85 launching sites for a far more agile missile, the SA-3. Effective at altitudes as low as 350 feet under optimum conditions, the SA-3 was designed to fill the gap between the high-reaching SA-2s and the 23-millimeter cannon of the ZSU-23. And no sooner were they in place than Egypt began deploying a still more dangerous missile—the SA-6, a 176-pound packet of high explosives and microchip circuitry then unsurpassed in ground-to-air defense. Mounted on a tracked carrier, it could follow behind an advancing armor or infantry battalion. Its two-stage radar guidance system—one antenna to search the skies for hostile planes, the other to steer the missile in flight—could pick up an approaching jet at a distance of 25 miles and send the missile to snatch it from the air. Should a target attempt to jam the radar on one frequency, the scanner would switch to another. Then, when the missile neared its target, a heat-seeking homing device took over. The SAM flew up the airplane's tailpipe and exploded. By the fall of 1973, the Egyptians had acquired 184 SA-6 launchers; Syria had 128.

Supplementing these heavy-duty SAMs, some Arab infantry companies carried the SA-7, a minimissile fired from the shoulder. Together, these weapons formed a web of antijet mayhem extending from near ground level to beyond the service ceiling of all Israeli jets. When the next war began, these defenses would all but deny Israel the edge that had brought victory in 1967—air supremacy over the battlefield.

Israeli intelligence experts loftily discounted what they knew of the Arab preparations. With the confidence of earlier triumph, Israel felt invincible. No Arab nation would dare attack. Occasional skirmishes in the air only stiffened this cavalier posture. When on September 13, 1973, a force of MiG-21s bounced an Israeli patrol off the Syrian coast, a fierce dogfight erupted in which a dozen Phantoms and Mirages downed 13 Syrian fighters, with a loss of only one Mirage. It stunningly confirmed the superiority of Israeli pilots, and of the planes they flew.

Sadat contributed to Israel's complacency. For more than a year he had been beating the drums of war, in speeches and radio broadcasts. But he had pounded too hard for too long; few believed he would really act. Then as summer passed into fall, Sadat's plans crystallized. Huge numbers of troops and tanks rolled up to the canal zone. Thousands of rubber rafts and pontoon bridge sections were buried in the dunes along the waterway. In Syria as well, infantry battalions were secretly mobilized; tanks were moved up and guns made ready.

October is a time of religious observance in the Middle East, with Ramadan, the month-long period of fasting in the Muslim world and with various high holy days in the Jewish faith. It is not a time for making war. On October 4, Sadat demobilized 20,000 troops. It was a ruse. Two days later, as Jews in Israel and around the world quietly celebrated Yom Kippur, their Day of Atonement, the Arabs struck.

Massed squadrons of Egyptian MiGs and Su-7 fighter-bombers, 250

The head-up display is mounted on the plane's front console, with dials for day or night brightness situated below.

A window on the pilot's world

The transparent glass screen in the F-15 Eagle cockpit at left is the jet's head-up display, or HUD, which allows the pilot to read critical flight information without ever taking his eyes off the action outside. Generated on a cathode-ray tube by a digital computer, the information is projected onto the screen as graphics, letters and numbers.

The diagram below reproduces the display in the photograph. The *W* in the center shows where the nose is pointed—toward 336 degrees, as read from the compass, or heading scale, on top. A small circle below and to the left of the *W* indicates flight direction, different from the heading because of a crosswind.

Passing through the small circle is the horizon line, part of a moving pitch scale represented by broken lines labeled *5*, which show the angle of the plane's nose to the horizon. On the vertical scale to the left, the notch indicates air speed, 285 knots (328 mph). Numbers below the scale give the speed as Mach .464 and the jet's rate of acceleration as 1.0G, a measure of the stress imposed on pilot and plane in a turn. To the right, a vertical scale shows altitude, 4,700 feet. The 11.6 at the lower right represents the time in minutes to the next radio navigation beacon along the plane's route.

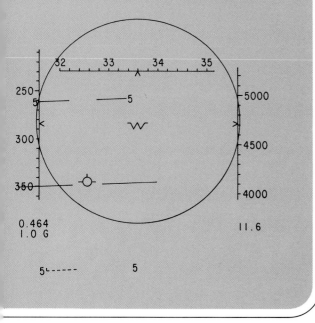

planes in all, swept over the canal to pound Israeli air bases, radar sites and missile batteries in the Sinai. At the same moment, 2:05 p.m., more than 2,000 heavy guns opened fire on Israel's Bar Lev Line. When the shelling stopped, assault troops crossed the canal in rubber rafts. Three and a half hours later they had overrun 14 Israeli strongpoints and hoisted Egypt's flag above the Sinai.

In the Golan Heights, Israel could muster fewer than 200 tanks to hold off 900 Syrian tanks. "I never knew there were so many tanks in all the world," said an Israeli armor commander.

During the early hours of the War, Israel made a basic strategic decision: While stalling the Egyptians in the Sinai, it would first stop the Syrians in the Golan Heights, where the battle surged to within 12 miles of Israel. Then, with the Syrians halted, it could confront the Egyptians as they rolled across the vast desert toward Israel.

To help hold the line while reserves were called up, Israel turned to the Air Force. By some happy instinct the air command had begun to take seriously intelligence reports of Egypt's build-up and earlier that day had started alerting pilots. Within half an hour of the assault, Phantoms and Skyhawks streamed west. They flew into a wall of missiles and flak that overwhelmed Israeli ECM. Ten jets took hits from a variety of SAMs in the first half hour and "plummeted to earth in flames," said an Egyptian commander, "as if they were falling comets." So terrible was the carnage that Israel's Chief of Staff, Lieutenant General David Elazar, prohibited flights within 10 miles of the canal, and losses declined.

In the Golan Heights, Israel's first defense priority, the toll was even heavier: 25 Skyhawks and five Phantoms shot down in just two hours. To limit losses, Israel's jets flew over Jordan and attacked the Syrian flank. Nevertheless, in the opening hours of the War, Israel had lost 40 aircraft—11 per cent of its fighters—along with many of its best pilots.

The SA-6 was especially nasty. "Once that thing gets behind you, it's all over," warned one pilot. A news correspondent on the Syrian front summed up the action: "It was a familiar sight to see the white spiral of an SA-6 in the blue sky . . . then a puff of grey smoke, and, before it had begun to disperse, there was the fast-falling flame of the shot-down Phantom. It was rare to see parachutes."

To neutralize the missiles, the Israelis first tried blitzing the SA-6 sites with near-suicidal dive-bombing attacks. Since the missile leaves the launcher at a relatively shallow angle to the ground, the assaulting Phantom would zoom up and then plunge down behind the SAM in an almost vertical dive to release its bombs or a radar-homing Shrike missile. But as often as not, because of the tight weave of the Arab air-defense nets, the jet would be hit by another SAM, or by a ZSU-23.

To evade the missiles, a pilot dived steeply and dropped decoy flares to spoof the SAM. With luck, the SA-6's infrared sensors would guide the missile to a flare rather than to the jet's tailpipe. Another Israeli decoy measure called for a flight leader to cross wakes with his wingman, thus creating a "hot spot" at the intersection point in hopes of detonating the missile prematurely. But when the missiles came in heavy salvos, as they often did, there was no way to outfly them.

Sudden help arrived from the United States. A massive airlift resupplied Israel with all manner of ammunition, tanks, artillery pieces and even aircraft. Among the treasures were newer, more effective ECM pods, along with large quantities of radar-confusing chaff. These devices foiled the older SAMs. But the chaff was not tailored to the SA-6 radar, which saw through it, and jamming the missile proved impossible. To be effective, ECM black boxes must be tuned to the transmitting frequency of a particular radar system. And for the SA-6, with its ability to switch channels, these frequencies were as yet unknown.

Early in the contest for the Golan Heights, as luck and skill would have it, Israeli jets knocked out the computer that controlled much of the Syrian missile screen. This created a relatively safe corridor through which the Phantoms and Skyhawks could drive unharmed to attack Syrian tanks and to chip away at the edges of the remaining missile net. It also allowed them to attack Damascus, the Syrian capital. The city's airport, which the Russians were using to resupply Syria, was a prime target, and Israeli Phantoms attacked it at dawn on the 14th.

"Beneath us Damascus valley seems to be boiling and steaming," reported an F-4 pilot who participated in the raid. "Missiles are flying through the air and AA shells are everywhere." But the missiles were SA-2s and SA-3s, and the pilot managed to evade them. He dropped his bombs on one of the airport's two runways, then as he and his squadronmates completed the run, a flight of MiGs dived down among them. The pilot recalled the excitement of the moment: "Everything is happening so fast! To the west I see a Phantom breaking left, with a MiG on its tail. I get behind them. If the MiG straightens its wings, I tell myself, I'll launch a missile at it."

As the MiG's wings straightened, the F-4 fired a Sidewinder—or an improved Israeli version called the Shafrir—and the voice of the back seater crackled over the earphones: "Break, you son of a bitch! Break!" A second MiG was moving in at 6 o'clock.

"He won't hit us," the Phantom pilot scoffed. "We're out of range."

But as he watched his missile strike the MiG ahead, cannon fire jolted his aircraft. The attacking MiG had found the range.

Another Phantom chased the MiG away before it could do further damage, but as the squadron continued toward Israel, the pilot of the crippled F-4 found himself skidding crazily in formation. When he landed he saw why: "a hole as big as a bucket" in his right wing tip.

The war with Syria was on the wane. Syria had begun to run short of SAMs. With Israel in control of the air, the battle for the Golan Heights soon turned in its favor. By October 15, the grand armada of Syrian tanks had been broken up, and Israel's troops had marched six miles into enemy territory. Israeli pilots had shot down more than 150 Syrian jets—roughly half that nation's Air Force.

With the Syrians thrown back, though hardly pacified, Israel turned to the Sinai, where the Egyptians had consolidated their positions. On October 14 the main Egyptian tank force had started east into the northern Sinai. The tanks were met—and stopped—by Israeli armor in a furious melee under an Israeli umbrella of Skyhawks and Phantoms. It was the War's second turning point.

The air battles over the Sinai were fierce and bloody. Egypt's pilots had toughened remarkably since 1967. One MiG-17 commander, Major Sherif Mohammed Arab, remembers sending four planes to shoot up Israeli tanks, then leading the remaining eight to bomb a nearby air base. They were jumped by eight Phantoms. A current of fear raced through Arab's brain: The F-4s were the most lethal aircraft in the Middle East; Israeli pilots were reputed to be all but invincible.

But as the MiGs and Phantoms clashed above the air base, Arab's mind cleared. "I saw from the way the Israelis maneuvered their planes that they were less experienced pilots than we had expected," he recalled. A Phantom bore in toward him, and he enticed it into a tight turning duel—left, reverse, then left again—each plane trying to close in behind the other. After a minute or two, Arab pulled back on his throttle and thrust out his speed brakes. The MiG hung in the air. The Phantom spurted ahead, and Arab lined up for the kill. "I shot him at a range of about 150 meters," he said. "I was astonished he didn't climb, because I could not have followed."

Top Egyptian pilots like Arab may have been a match for any foe, but they were too few to stop the generally superior Israeli pilots. The Phantoms, Skyhawks and Mirages averaged nearly 2,500 sorties a week against Egyptian forces in the Sinai. To keep losses down, they assiduously avoided the main SAM network between Cairo and the canal. To challenge the missiles meant certain destruction; the SAMs would have to be taken out by ground forces.

On October 16, in the single most daring action of the War, burly, fire-breathing Ariel Sharon sneaked a small detachment of tanks past the main force of Egypt's army in the Sinai and rafted them across the canal. Within hours, he had put seven SAM launchers out of action. In the next few days, Sharon reinforced his detachment on the west bank of the canal; by October 19, he had overrun as many as 40 launchers, enough to open a gaping hole in the Egyptian air defenses. Through this gap, which disrupted the overlapping coverage of SAM sites, Israel's jets began to score heavily against the ones that were left. Meanwhile, in a desolate pocket of the Sinai, 250 tanks and 20,000 men of Egypt's Third Army had been encircled and cut off from resupply. The men were slowly expiring from heat, thirst and incessant Israeli bombardment. On October 24, all sides agreed to a truce. Anwar Sadat's Yom Kippur adventure had failed to reclaim the Sinai.

More than five years later, after arduous negotiations, Egypt and Israel signed a formal peace accord. Under its provisions the Sinai was to be restored to Egypt, but that would not happen until late 1981, after Egypt

A true-to-life imitation of aerial combat

Inside a 40-foot domed simulator that resembles a planetarium, fighter pilots at McDonnell Douglas' St. Louis plant can get an astonishingly real sense of what it is like to be at the controls of the latest in jet aircraft. They do so in a cockpit that duplicates a plane's own sophisticated controls and electronic displays, with all the sights, sounds and other sensations of combat provided for verisimilitude.

The heart of the simulator is a high-speed computer, which controls several projectors that throw fast-moving images of earth and sky, planes and even incoming missiles onto the spherical screen. Thus, though the pilot is stationary, he has the illusion that he is flying. To complete the illusion, as he manipulates the controls to bank, the computer tilts the horizon. And when the pilot closes in on his target, the image automatically enlarges and the pressure on his G-suit increases, just as it would if he were actually accelerating. When he fires his gun or missiles and scores a hit, the enemy plane disappears from the screen.

Using the simulator, a pilot can complete 30 air-to-air or air-to-ground mock attacks in an hour, instead of the three possible in a real jet. The device enables him to test new features—and the manufacturer to refine them—before they are incorporated into the final design.

Seated in a cockpit from an F/A-18, a Navy pilot maneuvers alongside his wingman before closing in on a MiG-21, projected on the wall of the simulator at the McDonnell Douglas plant.

The cathode-ray tube on the far left indicates the kinds of missiles the pilot has at his disposal and which one—marked RDY, ready—the computer has selected for firing.

In a simulation of an air-to-ground attack, the pilot duplicates the maneuver of the F/A-18 in front of him and banks to approach a target. The image on the left cockpit display is a detailed television picture of the target area. In a real F/A-18, the so-called forward-looking infrared system, or FLIR, located in a pod on the fuselage, creates the image even during nighttime.

recognized Israel as a sovereign nation. Since no other Arab country made that concession, Israel kept the other occupied lands—the West Bank area of Jordan, the Golan Heights and the Gaza Strip—and confrontations continued: Israel against Syria, against Iraq and against the PLO, first in Jordan and later in Lebanon.

The advances in aerial weaponry during the 1970s exceeded those of any earlier decade. Three years after the Yom Kippur War, Sadat was still smarting at the superiority of Israel's Phantoms over his own MiG-21s. In the Israeli jets, he remarked during an interview with *The Times* of London, "everything is computerized for the pilot. If he enters a missile zone, there will be a lamp to tell him. If anyone is going to attack him from behind, another lamp will tell him. He just puts a card in the computer. It will take him to the place where he is going. It will tell him to drop the bomb. It will bring him back to his airport."

Flying an F-4 was not quite as easy as that, but Sadat had hit upon a basic truth of modern air warfare: To survive in an era of high speeds and superaccurate weapons, a pilot needed all the help he could get from his airplane. And a new generation of American jets—the F-14 Tomcat, the F-15 Eagle and the F-16 Fighting Falcon—would give it to him, proving so fast and agile that earlier fighters seemed rudimentary by comparison.

The genesis of these superplanes of the 1970s and 1980s went back nearly 20 years—to the emerging saga of Vietnam, and to an interim aircraft that was embroiled in controversy from its inception. The U.S. Department of Defense wanted an all-purpose plane to outduel any jet that tried to shoot it down. It also had to deliver bombs as reliably as the F-105 but take off in half the distance. It should have the latest in electronics to skim automatically a few hundred feet above mountainous terrain and find a target no matter how miserable the weather. The Defense Department, seeking a long production run to lower the cost of each jet, decreed that this new wonderplane should be the frontline fighter for both the Navy and the Air Force. The result—four years, six months and half a billion dollars later—was the General Dynamics F-111, a 50-ton monster that was promptly dubbed the Aardvark. Its most unusual feature was the variable-sweep wing. On takeoff and at low speeds, the wings spread wide. At high speeds they automatically swept back into a delta shape for optimum performance beyond Mach 1.

From the start, the Aardvark had problems. It was too unwieldy for dogfighting and far too big and heavy for the Navy's carriers. Its engines tended to lose power suddenly, and its smart new terrain-following radar often went awry. Gradually the new plane's mechanical troubles were eliminated, and the Aardvark became a reasonably effective all-weather attack aircraft. One version, the FB-111, was supplied to the Strategic Air Command as a nuclear bomber supplementing the B-52s. Nevertheless, the Navy and the Air Force each still needed a new fighter. So, using the research that had gone into creating the F-111, American aircraft manufacturers set to work. By the early 1970s, they had produced the two most formidable tactical jets in the world, aircraft that were intended to be the mainstay American fighters into the 1990s.

The Navy plane was Grumman's F-14 Tomcat, a twin-jet two-seater with variable-sweep wings like the F-111 and a top speed of Mach 2.34—1,560 miles per hour at 36,000 feet. The plane is most remarkable in its materials and construction. One fourth of the structure is made of titanium, a costly metal that withstands the heat of high-speed flight better than aluminum and also saves weight. To get rid of even more poundage, large areas of the stabilizer are fabricated of tough epoxy plastics strengthened with boron fibers.

Advanced avionics in the Tomcat give the pilot an edge in combat. The data he needs for fighting—distance to target and closing speed, what weapon is ready to fire and how many missiles and rounds of ammunition he has left—are projected at eye level in a so-called head-up display (HUD); the pilot's eyes need not leave the target. Besides a six-barrel cannon and radar-guided Phoenix and Sparrow missiles, the F-14 carries an improved model of the heat-seeking Sidewinder. It can be fired at a target from any angle, not just from behind; the missile is so sensitive that it can home in on the very friction of an enemy's fuselage sliding through the air. Indeed, when it appeared in 1972, the Tomcat seemed to have only one drawback: Each one cost about $17 million.

After nearly a decade with the U.S. Navy, the plane got a chance to prove itself. On August 19, 1981, two F-14s from the carrier *Nimitz,* conducting an exercise in the Gulf of Sidra off Libya, intercepted two Soviet-built Sukhoi Su-22s, piloted by Libyans and headed toward the ship. Thirty-five such incidents had occurred the preceding day with a variety of Libyan jets, but the planes had either turned away or been escorted by the F-14s as they maneuvered close to the *Nimitz.*

This occasion was different. One of the Libyan jets fired a missile head on at the lead Tomcat from a range of 1,000 feet. Commander Henry Kleeman, the pilot, and Lieutenant Lawrence Muczynski, flying the second F-14, evaded the missile by turning sharply to port. The U.S. permits its fighters to shoot back if fired upon, so each of the Navy pilots positioned his Tomcat behind one of the Libyan jets. Kleeman was ready with a Sidewinder but could not fire immediately; his target was headed directly into the sun, a hot spot that would have confused the heat-seeking missile. As soon as the Su-22 turned away from the sun, Kleeman fired. When the missile struck the Libyan plane, the pilot ejected; he was later rescued by his countrymen. At the same moment, Muczynski squeezed off a Sidewinder at the second assailant. The missile flew into the Su-22's tailpipe and exploded, breaking the jet in two. No parachute was seen.

The new Air Force fighter was the single-seat McDonnell Douglas F-15 Eagle. It, too, took advantage of the latest in materials and weapons systems, though it had fixed wings and carried no Phoenix missiles.

What distinguished the Eagle from its Navy cousin was the immense power of its engines, two compact Pratt & Whitney F-100 jets that

Britain's marvelous jump jet

As Mach 2 speeds become ever more common in jet fighters, the RAF Harrier, with a modest cruising speed of 690 mph, bears out a veteran pilot's assertion that "mobility, flexibility and surprise are still as important as they ever were."

The Pegasus engine at the heart of the Harrier gives the little fighter a potent agility. By moving a lever located alongside the throttle, the pilot can vary the direction of engine thrust and make the plane rise straight up, hover and maneuver forward or backward, then land vertically on an area 60 feet in diameter.

The advantages of such a plane are many. Large, easily targeted airfields become unnecessary; in wartime, Harriers can hide in camouflage tents close to combat, ready to leap into battle. At sea, they can operate from relatively small, economical carriers. And because, as a Harrier pilot said, it is "far better to stop and land, than land and try to stop," the jets take off and return far more safely than conventional aircraft. Aloft, vectoring engine thrust at critical moments enables the Harrier to outmaneuver challengers, as it pitches instantly into a sharp turn or decelerates so rapidly that, in the words of one flier, "you think you are stopping at 12,000 feet."

Proof that the Harrier can be more than a match for faster fighters came in late spring of 1982, when 38 Harriers and Sea Harriers were dispatched to the South Atlantic to fly air defense, reconnaissance and ground attack in the war to retake the Falkland Islands. Flying in weather that would have kept conventional aircraft lashed to the flight decks, British Harrier pilots downed a total of 31 Argentine jets—among them 19 supersonic French-built Mirages—without a single loss of their own in air combat.

Headed for Falkland Sound in May 1982, a Sea Harrier takes off from a ski-jump launch ramp used to boost the plane's payload.

Diagrams of two effective dogfight tactics show how a Harrier pilot (blue plane) vectors engine thrust to gain the advantage over faster but less maneuverable aircraft. At the top of an arcing climb (above), the pilot shifts the direction of thrust to vertical and the plane plunges straight down to the inside position, making the enemy its target. Angling thrust slightly while inverted in a steep climb (right), he flips the Harrier into a sharp dive, then reverses thrust and slows the jet while the enemy hurtles into range.

The exhaust nozzles of this Rolls-Royce Pegasus engine point down for vertical takeoff or landing. The nozzles can rotate along a 98-degree arc, from fully aft for conventional flight to eight degrees forward of vertical for braking.

pound for pound generated more thrust, with less expenditure of fuel, than any other type. Together their thrust was greater than the weight of the plane fully loaded for combat. Pilots of an earlier day often spoke of forcing their birds into a vertical climb; they were exaggerating. The F-86 could achieve perhaps a 45-degree angle; the F-4 about 70 degrees. The Eagle could stand on its tail and rocket straight up into the sky, accelerating to supersonic speed as it went. It could climb to 60,000 feet—more than 11 miles up—in two minutes. On the deck, the Eagle was agile enough to outmaneuver any Soviet jet.

At $6.5 million, the cost of each F-15 was bearable when the plane was introduced in 1970. But the price rocketed upward, and the F-15 soon became too expensive for the Air Force to equip all its fighter wings with them. The General Dynamics F-16 Fighting Falcon filled in admirably. In some ways it was the most extraordinary aircraft of all.

The F-16 was compact (wingspan 33 feet), light (only 15,600 pounds without fuel or armament) and relatively inexpensive (a bargain in 1975 at more than five million dollars), and it had lines so clean that they seemed to melt into the air itself. Though the Falcon's avionics and ECM gear were less elaborate than either the Tomcat's or the Eagle's, it was in other respects even more computerized.

In most jets, the connection between the pilot's controls and the rudder, elevators and ailerons was hydraulic, as in a car with power steering. But in the F-16, the link was electronic. Computers sensed the pilot's slightest pressure on the stick and instantly commanded the aircraft to turn, climb or dive. Not only did this "fly-by-wire" system respond more precisely, but its electronic circuits were less vulnerable than hydraulic lines to gunfire and near misses from missiles. The Falcon could fly circles around any other modern jet, including the newest generation of MiGs. And should the F-16 be pressed into service for ground attacks, it could haul its own weight in bombs.

In the past, the U.S. had rarely sold its most advanced fighters abroad, but the policy changed in the 1970s. Foreign sales meant that more planes would be built, lowering the cost of each. Among the first in line was Israel, which ordered 48 Eagles and 75 Falcons.

Meanwhile, Egypt and Syria had been modernizing their Air Forces with small numbers of the latest aircraft from the Soviet Union. To complement the MiG-21 fair-weather fighter, the Russians had designed the MiG-23, a Mach 2 swing-wing all-weather interceptor, and a somewhat slower ground-attack version of the same plane, designated the MiG-27. Both jets mounted a potent assortment of guided missiles.

For years after the Yom Kippur War, no violence occurred that compared with it, but neither was there peace. The tension had become centered in Lebanon, where Muslim and Christian factions battled each other in a stop-and-go civil war, and where the PLO was free to operate as a state within a state, with its own army. In 1976 Syria, on the pretext of restoring order, moved 20,000 troops into the valleys east of Beirut. Under cover of the general chaos, the Palestinians stepped up their terrorist raids into Israel and began throwing in shells from artillery near the border.

The Israelis replied by bombing and strafing PLO installations. Rarely did Syrian MiGs respond, but when they did, the result could be a fierce dogfight. Thus it was that on June 27, 1979, the F-15 Eagle scored its first kill. There were six Eagles and two Kfirs—souped-up, Israeli-built versions of the French Mirage V, with an American engine—against more than eight Syrian MiG-19s. In just short of five minutes, Israel claimed, five MiGs lay splattered across the landscape; the rest got away, at least two of them badly crippled. Israel reported no losses.

Even clearer proof of the F-15's virtues—and of the Israelis' skill at applying them—occurred two years later, 500 miles to the east, in Iraq.

The Iraqis had almost finished building a $260 million nuclear reactor in the desert 11 miles southwest of Baghdad. Its declared purpose was atomic research for peacetime uses. But despite assurances from France, which had provided the reactor, and the safeguard of surprise visits from the U.N.'s nuclear watchdog, the International Atomic Energy Agency, Israel suspected the worst: The reactor was a type that would produce as a by-product the kind of uranium used for nuclear bombs. Israel resolved not to let one of her most implacable enemies acquire the means to build such a weapon, especially after Iraq's official newspaper reported that Iraq's intention was to do so.

An air strike was the only practical remedy, and plans for it had been evolving over many months. For example, Israel's Air Force had built in the desert a full-scale model of the reactor complex and was running practice bomb attacks against it. By the spring of 1981, the Israelis were ready for the real thing. And just in time. The Iraqi reactor would begin operating in a matter of weeks. It would then be so radioactive that bombing it would expose all of Baghdad to nuclear radiation.

On Sunday, June 7, 1981, at 4:40 in the afternoon, six missile-armed F-15s took off from Etzion air base in the Sinai and headed east; they would provide top cover for the main strike force should Iraq send up any of its 80 MiG-23 interceptors. Eight F-16 Falcons followed close behind. The lead Falcon carried two video-guided "smart" bombs; five others each had a pair of 2,200-pound unguided blockbusters, with delayed-action fuses, and two carried cameras rather than bombs.

The force swept east in a zigzag course over Saudi Arabia near the Jordanian border. The F-16s, by keeping low and weaving back and forth, escaped detection by Arab radar. But the higher-flying F-15s were picked up by a radar scanner in southern Jordan. The Israelis had anticipated such a complication, and to the Jordanian radio challenge the flight leader answered in perfect Arabic, convincing the operator that he was part of a Jordanian air patrol.

At 5:30, with the afternoon sun casting long, knifelike shadows across the desert, the Israelis sighted the reactor's cupola rising above the sands. The lead Falcon pilot aimed his video-guided bombs at a predetermined spot on the cupola, punching jagged, gaping holes through

On the HUD, computer graphics plot a safe route through antiaircraft defenses. Here, two SAM sites threaten a fighter. A battery in the yellow zone is not yet tracking the plane and is less of a threat than the one in the red zone. This site has locked onto the jet and can hit it if the plane holds the course indicated by the circle at the center of the display. To avoid both sites, the computer flies the craft from one numbered signpost to another on a path just above the checkered pattern representing the ground.

Flying by computer and a television screen

In tomorrow's jet fighter, a pilot will rely more than ever on computer-generated displays to give him the information he needs to fly a mission.

At the touch of a button on the throttle stick or instrument panel, he will be able to call up on TV screens and a head-up display any flight information he needs—speed and heading, engine RPM, tailpipe temperature, how much fuel he has left. In case of a malfunction or an emergency, a warning will auto-matically appear, overriding less crucial information. Dials and gauges will no longer clutter the cockpit; only a few will be retained as backups.

In combat, the pilot will be able to choose from a variety of sensors—in-cluding radar, low-light-level TV and an infrared-imaging system *(below)*—for a clear picture of his target, even at night. If he wishes, his computer will analyze data it collects about enemy defenses and project a path to safety on the HUD *(left)*.

A pilot's-eye view of the cockpit of the future shows five separate images. The one on the right is of the target, a bridge, with the pipper on it. The center picture is a close-up of the bridge; a small TV camera mounted on the nose of a "smart" missile provides the view. In the graphic display at left the missile is colored green and marked RDY—ready to fire. The map being flashed on the screen between the pilot's knees reveals that the aircraft will automatically escape to the right after firing the missile.

the thick concrete. The next plane swooped in, and the next, each pilot releasing his bombs with such precision that they fell through the original holes to detonate inside. Seconds later the bombs exploded, and with a shattering roar the dome collapsed, burying the reactor core under hundreds of tons of rubble. One person, a French technician, was working at the facility that Sunday, and he was killed instantly. He was the raid's only casualty. Puffs of flak from a nearby antiaircraft gun dotted the wakes of the retreating strike planes but caused no harm. Not a single MiG appeared, and all the planes returned safely. Israel's air chief, Major General David Ivri, pronounced the raid a total success. "There was not one incident during the entire operation which we didn't anticipate," he said. "It was boring."

But the rest of the world was in an uproar. The Israelis, even their friends said, had stepped brazenly out of bounds. "I am saddened," declared French Foreign Minister Claude Cheysson. "We don't think such action serves the cause of peace in the area." Britain's outspoken Prime Minister Margaret Thatcher called it "a grave breach of international law." And U.S. President Ronald Reagan suspended Israel's next shipment of F-16s.

And the conflict continued. Back in April of 1981, a flight of Israeli jets had roared over the Bekaa valley, east of Beirut, where "peace-keeping" Syrian forces were trading potshots with Christian militiamen allied with Israel; the Israelis downed two Syrian helicopters. The Syrians responded by wheeling in SA-6 missiles. PLO soldiers were staging an attack inside Israel nearly every other day. After 130 such incidents in nine months, Israel launched a full-scale invasion to expel the PLO from Lebanon. Sixty thousand troops and 500 tanks pushed across the border in the wake of air strikes by F-4s, Kfirs, F-15s and F-16s.

Since the last time Israelis had faced the SA-6, they had found the key to defeating it. They sent in unmanned drones with TV cameras and tape recorders to pinpoint the launchers and monitor their radar emissions; then the strike planes, their ECM boxes set to counter the radar, could bomb and rocket their targets unmolested.

On the afternoon of June 9, Eagles, Falcons and Kfirs—90 of them—howled across the Bekaa valley and hit the launchers. Syrian MiGs rose to defend the SAM sites but failed utterly. Radar aboard an Israeli E-2C Hawkeye, an airborne command center with many of the same capabilities as its larger cousin the AWACS *(pages 142-145)*, spotted the MiGs as they took off, so that they could be handily intercepted. What is more, the Syrian pilots fought listlessly. They behaved, according to one Israeli account, "as if they knew they were going to be shot down and waited to see when it was going to happen." By the end of the day, nearly half of the 60 Syrian warplanes sent up to meet the Israelis were black smears on the valley floor; and Israel's jets had obliterated 60 SA-6 launchers in the valley. Not a single Israeli aircraft was lost. Though most of the SAMs in the valley had been knocked out, dogfights continued almost unabated for the next two days; Syria sacrificed 50 more aircraft in a vain attempt to challenge the Israelis. In the next weeks, as the aerial contest wound down, the total of Syrian losses in air-to-air combat would rise to 85. Not one Syrian pilot scored a kill.

Then the jets turned on Beirut. Over the years, the PLO had set up headquarters and cached substantial quantities of arms and munitions in the Muslim west side of the city. Air strikes reduced suspected PLO buildings to ruins. And once again it seemed that Israel had overstepped the bounds of reasonable retaliation. Often there were people inside the damaged buildings who had no connection with the PLO. Sometimes the bombs missed the target and hit adjacent apartment houses, and in one case a hospital. Civilian casualties numbered in the hundreds.

Israel, with diplomatic aid from the U.S., succeeded in evicting the PLO soldiers from Beirut and dispersing them throughout the Arab world. But peace between Israel and its foes seemed as elusive as ever.

Circumstances may occur that require a nation's air force to be its first line of defense against aggressors. It is safe to forecast that future fighting jets will show vast improvements over today's. Already the U.S. Air Force is evaluating a modified F-16 Falcon that has two winglets, or canards, slanting downward from the fuselage. With this feature, the F-16 can scoot sideways to dodge a missile or to spoil the aim of a pursuing pilot. A new wing has been proposed for the plane that somewhat resembles a delta wing in shape. It would decrease the F-16's takeoff run, increase fuel capacity and raise the plane's low-altitude speed by about 100 miles per hour.

In the near future, the strong, reinforced plastics used in aircraft construction may lead to wings that are swept forward rather than back for better low-speed stability. So-called stealth aircraft promise to be difficult to detect by radar: The same plastics, formed into aircraft components that have been subtly shaped and covered with special paints to reflect radar beams less readily, will act like a cloak of invisibility.

Improvements in cockpits will enable a pilot to devote all his attention to reaching a target safely, destroying it and getting away to fight again; a computer, as Anwar Sadat ruefully complained in 1976, will now actually fly the plane. New head-up displays (pages 150-151) will make the HUDs of the early 1980s seem as old-fashioned as the vintage A-1 radar gun sight of the Korean War Sabre jet. A fighter pilot may even be able to speak to his aircraft. Experiments are under way to determine whether jet fighters can be "taught" to recognize and execute simple voice commands—to ready a weapon, for example, or to turn or climb.

Yet all such advances are simply refinements of the basic ingredients of aerial combat—a skilled and aggressive pilot guiding his aircraft through a hostile sky. In the next battle, as in the past, flak will rend the air with red-hot shrapnel. Missiles will draw smoke trails helter-skelter in the sky as they ferret out their victims. And at any moment a pilot may hear an urgent call from his wingman: "Break right, Lead, break! Bandit at your 6 o'clock!"

Modern marvels of aerial might

During the 1970s, jet fighters became increasingly versatile. Experience in Vietnam and the Middle East clearly confirmed the need for planes that could quickly shift from aerial-combat to ground-attack missions. These bitter conflicts—and the spiraling costs of new weapons systems— eroded the conventional distinction between pure interceptors and fighter-bombers. Thus, with the exception of the MiG-25 *(above)* and the Fairchild A-10 *(page 168)*, all the jets in this picture essay were designed from the start to fly and fight as true multirole combat aircraft.

The search for flexibility spawned some surprising technical innovations. The Saab Viggen *(right)* was fitted with canards, or winglets, near the nose for better low-speed handling; on the Grumman F-14 and the MiG-23, that goal was achieved with variable-sweep wings. Electronic "fly-by-wire" controls and lightweight carbon-fiber structures in McDonnell Douglas' F-16 and Dassault's Mirage 2000 contributed to these planes' unprecedented combat maneuverability; the Yak-36 utilized three separate jet engines for vertical takeoffs and landings from small carriers and ships. The dates each plane entered service are noted in parentheses and planes on adjacent pages are in scale.

MIKOYAN-GUREVICH MIG-25P (1970)
Code-named "Foxbat-A" by the NATO allies, this heavy, twin-engined Soviet interceptor was for a time thought to be more advanced than anything in the Western arsenal. It boasts a top speed of 2,100 mph, but it is shorter-ranged and far less maneuverable than the American F-15. The plane shown bears the markings of the Soviet PVO Strany air-defense force and carries four AA-6 "Acrid" air-to-air missiles.

SAAB JA37 VIGGEN (1971)
Produced in air-superiority, ground-attack and reconnaissance versions, this nimble Mach 2 fighter can operate from very short airstrips or stretches of highway. The interceptor version that is shown here in the brown-and-green camouflage of the Swedish Air Force carries two Sky Flash and two Sidewinder air-to-air missiles.

GRUMMAN F-14A TOMCAT (1972)
*One of the world's outstanding combat
aircraft, this two-seat carrierborne fighter
has computer-controlled variable-sweep
wings and an advanced radar that can
simultaneously track 24 targets and direct
attacks against any six of them at a
distance of up to 100 miles. Armed with a
20-mm. multibarrel cannon and a mix of
Sparrow, Sidewinder and Phoenix air-to-air
missiles, the F-14 shown here belongs to
the U.S. Navy's Fighter Squadron 41.*

MIKOYAN-GUREVICH MIG-23S (1973)

This Soviet single-seat, all-weather interceptor, code-named "Flogger-B" by NATO, has a variable-sweep wing similar to the F-14's and avionics comparable to those of the earlier F-4 Phantom. A 25,350-pound-thrust afterburning turbofan engine gives it a top speed of 1,319 mph and a range of 620 miles. It carries a 23-mm. cannon and four air-to-air missiles.

MCDONNELL DOUGLAS F-15C EAGLE (1974)

A versatile air-superiority fighter, the all-weather Eagle also has a formidable ground-attack capability. Powered by twin 23,180-pound-thrust Pratt & Whitney engines, the Eagle flies at a top speed of more than 1,650 mph and carries eight Sidewinder and Sparrow missiles in addition to its 20-mm. cannon. Israeli Air Force Eagles proved deadly against Syrian MiGs in the 1982 Bekaa valley campaign. This craft belongs to the USAF's 36th Tactical Fighter Wing, stationed at Bitburg, West Germany.

FAIRCHILD-REPUBLIC A-10 THUNDERBOLT II (1976)
*The A-10's heavily armored fuselage is built
around a rapid-firing, tank-busting 30-mm.
cannon that is the most powerful gun ever
installed in an aircraft. The twin 9,065-
pound-thrust turbofan engines are mounted
aft on pylons for maximum protection
against ground fire; they give the plane a top
speed of 518 mph and a load-carrying
capacity of 16,000 pounds of bombs. The
A-10 shown here bears the shark's mouth of
the USAF's 23rd Tactical Fighter Wing.*

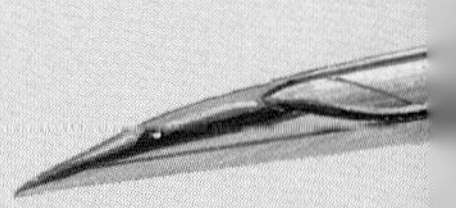

YAKOVLEV YAK-36 (1975)
*Code-named "Forger-A" by NATO, the
Yak-36 is a shipborne multirole fighter
that can take off and land vertically. Unlike
the single-engined British Harrier, it
makes only partial use of vectored thrust; a
forward pair of 8,000-pound-thrust jets
angled downward provides vertical lift, while
a larger, 17,600-pound-thrust engine
with two rotating nozzles lifts the rear and
propels the plane in level flight.*

DASSAULT-BREGUET SUPER ETENDARD (1978)
This French-built naval strike plane won worldwide attention in 1982 when a Super Etendard operated by the Argentine Navy sank a British destroyer off the Falkland Islands. Powered by an 11,265-pound-thrust engine, it has a top speed of 745 mph and a range of 1,243 miles. The plane depicted here, belonging to France's Aéronavale, carries the same Exocet air-to-surface antiship missiles used in the Falklands attack.

DASSAULT-BREGUET MIRAGE 2000 (1982)
*Dassault's delta-winged Mirage 2000
emerged from a government-sponsored
program aimed at incorporating advanced
technology in fighter design. Electronic
"fly-by-wire" flight controls make it
extraordinarily agile, and a 19,840-pound-
thrust engine gives it a top speed of 1,510
mph. The plane shown here, armed with
twin 30-mm. cannon and four Matra air-to-
air missiles, is the fourth prototype.*

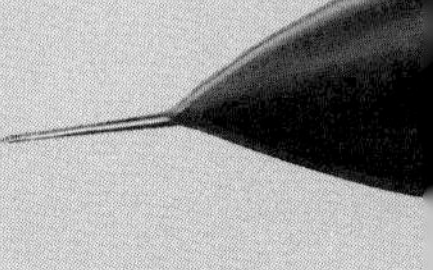

GENERAL DYNAMICS F-16A FIGHTING FALCON (1978)
*Originally designed as a smaller, cheaper
fighter to supplement the F-15, the Falcon
quickly became famous for its superb
handling. It has a top speed of 1,300 mph
and carries a 20-mm. cannon and Sidewinder
missiles. By 1983, eight countries were
operating the plane; this one belongs to the
USAF's 388th Tactical Fighter Wing.*

PANAVIA TORNADO IDS (1982)
A joint product of British, West German and Italian industry, the Tornado is a multirole all-weather fighter. Powered by two 15,000-pound-thrust engines and with a top speed of 1,320 mph, it carries two 27-mm. cannon and up to 18,000 pounds of bombs; an air-defense version is also produced for the RAF. The plane above bears the Iron Cross insignia of the West German Luftwaffe.

Acknowledgments

The index for this book was prepared by Gale Linck Partoyan. For their valuable help in the preparation of this volume, the editors wish to thank: **In Egypt:** Cairo—Lieutenant Colonel Sherif Mohammed Arab, Lieutenant Colonel Mohammed Dia el-Hefnawy, Egyptian Air Force. **In the Federal Republic of Germany:** Babenhausen—Heinz J. Nowarra; Berlin (West)—Wolfgang Streubel, Ullstein Bilderdienst; Bonn—General Adolf Galland (Ret.); Koblenz—Meinrad Nilges, Bundesarchiv; Königsbrunn/Augsburg—Hanfried Schliephake; Mainz-Finthen—Karl Ries; Munich—Hans Ebert, Messerschmitt-Bölkow-Blohm; Walter Zucker, Deutsches Museum. **In France:** Ivry-sur-Seine—Georges Roland, E.C.P. Armées; Le Bourget—Georges Delaleau, Yvan Kayser, Général Pierre Lissarague, Director, Stéphane Nicolaou, Général Roger de Ruffray, Deputy-Director, Colonel Pierre Willefert, Curator, Musée de l'Air; Paris—Avions Marcel Dassault; Michel Bénichou, *Le Fanatique de l'Aviation;* Paul Lengellé; Saint-Sever-sur-Adour—Jean-Jacques Petit; Toulouse—Patrick Laureau. **In the German Democratic Republic:** Berlin (DDR)—Hannes Quaschinsky, ADN-Zentralbild. **In Great Britain:** Bath—P. T. Barnard, Military Gallery; Bristol—Ernest Brook, Rolls-Royce Ltd.; Gloucester—Derek James; London—Denis Bateman, Air Historical Branch, Ministry of Defence; Yvonne Bonham, Guild of Aviation Artists; Matthew Nathan; Reginald Mack, Richard Simpson, RAF Museum; Bruce Robertson; John Bagley, Andrew Namum, Science Museum; Alan Williams, Imperial War Museum; Marjorie Willis, BBC Hulton Picture Library. **In Israel:** Israeli Air Force; Tel Aviv—Brigadier General (Reserve) A. Yalo Shavit. **In the Union of Soviet Socialist Republics:** Moscow—Soviet Copyright Agency. **In the United States:** Alabama—Lieutenant Colonel John F. Guilmartin Jr., Editor, Major Earl H. Tilford Jr., Associate Editor, *Air University Review,* Maxwell Air Force Base; Washington, D.C.—Captain M. Susan Cober, Historian, Office of Air Force History, Bolling Air Force Base; Julie Gustafson, Researcher, Air Force Depository, Bolling Air Force Base; Alice Price, Art Museum Branch, the Pentagon; G. Wesley Pryce, Historian, Naval Historical Center, Washington Navy Yard; Edmund T. Wooldridge, Curator, Department of Aeronautics, National Air and Space Museum; Missouri—E. Gene Adam, Staff Manager, MDC Fellow, Advanced Crew Systems, McDonnell Douglas Corporation; Jeffrey L. Fister, Associate External Relations Writer, Larry Ross, Branch Chief, Flight Simulation, McDonnell Douglas Corporation; Nebraska—Captain Tom Hall, Headquarters, SAC/PAM, Offutt Air Force Base; New York—Russell Burrows, Larry Burrows Collection; Virginia—Virginia Bader; Jay A. Erwin, Branch Head, Weapons Training Division, Naval Air Systems Command; Joe Pica, Boeing Company; Lieutenant Colonel Eric Solander, Chief, Magazines and Books Division, Department of the Air Force.

Bibliography

Books

Bonds, Ray, ed., *The Vietnam War: The Illustrated History of the Conflict in Southeast Asia.* Crown, 1979.

Boyne, Walter J.:
Boeing B-52: A Documentary History. London: Jane's, 1981.
Messerschmitt Me 262: Arrow to the Future. Smithsonian Institution Press, 1980.

Boyne, Walter J., and Donald S. Lopez, *The Jet Age: Forty Years of Jet Aviation.* National Air and Space Museum, Smithsonian Institution, 1979.

Churchill, Randolph S. and Winston S., *The Six Day War.* Houghton Mifflin, 1967.

Davis, Larry, *MIG Alley.* Squadron/Signal, 1978.

Dupuy, Colonel Trevor N., *Elusive Victory: The Arab-Israeli Wars, 1947-1974.* Harper & Row, 1978.

Eshel, Lt. Col. David, *The Israeli Air Force: Born in Battle.* Israel: Dramit, 1978.

Ethell, Jeffrey, and Alfred Price, *The German Jets in Combat.* London: Jane's, 1979.

Futrell, Robert Frank, *The United States Air Force in Korea 1950-1953.* Duell, Sloan and Pearce, 1961.

Galland, Adolf, *The First and the Last.* Henry Holt, 1954.

Green, William, *The Warplanes of the Third Reich.* Doubleday, 1970.

Gunston, Bill, *The Illustrated Encyclopedia of the World's Modern Military Aircraft.* Crescent Books, 1977.

Herzog, Chaim, *The Arab-Israeli Wars: War and Peace in the Middle East.* Random House, 1982.

Higham, Robin, and Jacob W. Kipp, eds., *Soviet Aviation and Air Power: A Historical View.* Westview Press, 1978.

Hopkins, J. C., *The Development of Strategic Air Command 1946-1981: A Chronological History.* Office of the Historian, Strategic Air Command, 1982.

Jackson, Robert:
Air War over Korea. Charles Scribner's Sons, 1973.
The Jet Age: True Tales of the Air since 1945. St. Martin's Press, 1980.

LeMay, General Curtis E., with MacKinlay Kantor, *Mission with LeMay: My Story.* Doubleday, 1965.

Lewy, Guenter, *America in Vietnam.* New York: Oxford University Press, 1978.

MacLeish, Roderick, *The Sun Stood Still.* Atheneum, 1967.

Mason, Herbert Molloy, Jr., *The United States Air Force: A Turbulent History.* Mason/Charter, 1976.

Mersky, Peter B., and Norman Polmar, *The Naval Air War in Vietnam.* The Nautical and Aviation Publishing Company of America, 1981.

Moss, Norman, *Men Who Play God: The Story of the H-Bomb and How the World Came to Live with It.* Harper & Row, 1968.

O'Ballance, Edgar, *No Victor, No Vanquished: The Yom Kippur War.* Presidio Press, 1978.

Polmar, Norman, ed., *Strategic Air Command: People, Aircraft, and Missiles.* The Nautical and Aviation Publishing Company of America, 1979.

Rubenstein, Murray, and Richard Goldman, *Shield of David: An Illustrated History of the Israeli Air Force.* Prentice-Hall, 1978.

Scutts, J. C., *F-105 Thunderchief.* Charles Scribner's Sons, 1981.

Smith, J. R., and Antony L. Kay, *German Aircraft of the Second World War.* Putnam, 1972.

Stevenson, James Perry, *Grumman F-14 "Tomcat."* Aero Publishers, 1975.

Szulc, Tad, *The Bombs of Palomares.* Viking, 1967.

Taylor, John W. R., ed., *Combat Aircraft of the World from 1909 to the Present.* G. P. Putnam's Sons, 1969.

Wagner, Ray, *The North American Sabre.* Doubleday, 1963.

White, William L., *The Little Toy Dog: The Story of the Two RB-47 Flyers, Captain John R. McKone and Captain Freeman B. Olmstead.* E. P. Dutton, 1962.

Picture credits

The sources for the illustrations that appear in this book are listed below. Credits for the illustrations from left to right are separated by semicolons; from top to bottom they are separated by dashes.
Endpaper (and cover detail, regular edition): Painting by Frank Wootton. 6, 7: Painting by Frank Wootton. 8, 9: Painting by R. G. Smith, courtesy McDonnell Douglas Corp. 10, 11: Painting by R. G. Smith, courtesy U.S. Navy. 12, 13: Painting by R. G. Smith, courtesy McDonnell Douglas Corp. 14, 15: Painting by William S. Phillips, courtesy Virginia Bader Fine Arts; painting by Frank Wootton. 16, 17: Painting by R. G. Smith, courtesy McDonnell Douglas Corp. 18, 19: U.S. Air Force. 21: Courtesy Heinz J. Nowarra, Babenhausen. 23: ADN-Zentralbild, Berlin (DDR). 24: Messerschmitt-Bölkow-Blohm, Munich. 26: Archiv Werner Held, Ransbach-Baumbach. 29: Archiv Werner Held, Ransbach-Baumbach—Deutsches Museum, Munich. 30: Courtesy Heinz J. Nowarra, Babenhausen—Messerschmitt-Bölkow-Blohm. 31: General Adolf Galland (Ret.), Bonn—courtesy Heinz J. Nowarra, Babenhausen. 32: U.S. Air Force—courtesy Günther F. Heise, Munich—Bundesarchiv, Koblenz. 34: Bundesarchiv, Koblenz. 35: Archiv Werner Held, Ransbach-Baumbach. 36: Courtesy Heinz J. Nowarra, Babenhausen. 37: Deutsches Museum, Munich. 38: Painting by Frank Wootton. 41: Deutsches Museum, Munich. 42-44: U.S. Air Force. 47: National Archives (Neg. No. 80-G-432622). 49: U.S. Air Force. 51: Map by Bill Hezlep. 52, 53: U.S. Air Force. 57-60: Drawings by John Amendola Studio. 63-71: U.S. Air Force. 72, 73: U.S. Air Force from Squadron Signal Publications. 74-77: U.S. Air Force. 78: A. Y. Owen. 79: Map by Bill Hezlep. 80, 81: Margaret Bourke-White for *Life*. 84, 85: Ralph Crane for *Life*. 88, 89: Michael Rougier for *Life*. 90: Rockwell International Corp.—*Air Force Magazine*. 94: Robert Kelley for *Life*. 96-101: Drawings by John Amendola Studio. 102: Larry Burrows. 105: Larry Burrows for *Life*. 107: Map by Walter Roberts. 108, 109: Larry Burrows for *Life*. 111, 113: U.S. Air Force. 114, 115: Larry Burrows for *Life*—U.S. Air Force (3). 116: © Marc Riboud, Paris. 119-122: Larry Burrows for *Life*. 126, 127: Nancy Moran. 128, 129: Nancy Moran; Wide World—Nancy Moran. 130, 131: U.S. Navy; Wide World—UPI. 132, 133: UPI. 134: Micha Bar-Am from Magnum. 136: © Cornell Capa from Magnum. 137: Paul Schutzer for *Life*. 138, 139: Keystone Press. 141: Boeing Company. 142, 143: Drawings by Rob Wood, Stansbury, Ronsaville, Wood Inc. 146, 148: George Hall. 149: Chart by Frederic F. Bigio from B-C Graphics. 152, 153: McDonnell Douglas Corp. 156: Lieutenant Commander Rupert Nichol, Fleet Air Arm Museum, Yeovilton, England. 157: Drawings by Rob Wood, Stansbury, Ronsaville, Wood Inc.—Rolls-Royce Ltd., Bristol. 160, 161: McDonnell Douglas Corp. 164-171: Drawings by John Amendola Studio.

Index